TRAILS
OF TEARS

American Indians Driven

From Their Lands

D0955539

TRAILS
OF TEARS

American Indians Driven

From Their Lands

Jeanne Williams

Hendrick-Long Publishing Co.

Dallas, Texas

For

David and Jason

with love

Library of Congress Cataloging-in-Publication Data
Williams, Jeanne, 1930-
   Trails of tears : American Indians driven from their lands /
Jeanne Williams.
     p. cm.
   Includes bibliographical references and index.
   Summary: Describes the white man's treatment and forcible dis-
placement of five Indian nations of the Southwest—the Comanche,
Cheyenne, Apache, Navajo, and Cherokee.
   ISBN 0-937460-76-1
   1. Indians of North America—Removal. 2. Indians of North
America—Government relations. [1. Indians of North America—
History.] I. Title.
E98.R4W55   1992
973'.0497—dc20   91-28549
                                                   CIP
                                                   AC

Hendrick-Long Publishing Company
Dallas, Texas 75225-1123

MAIN

CONTENTS

MAPS

FOREWORD

Americans are descendants of survivors of persecution or hardship in their homelands—survivors of voyages as different as those of the *Mayflower* and slave ships out of Africa.

There also is another group of American descendants of survivors—Indians who suffered the seizure of their lands by strangers and endured soul-bruising, body-maiming forced migrations.

This book cannot be a comprehensive history of each Native American tribe mentioned, much less a record of how the United States dealt with all of them. It shows how five different tribes lived through forcible uprootings and how they have adapted. It also gives some hint of the wide diversity of Indian cultures.

Tribal experience with the whites depended on the desirability of their land, their temperament and way of life, and whether their living patterns could survive in the white man's world.

A fortunate handful like the Tohono O'odham

and Zuñi have stayed on their ancestral lands, though the white man's increasing greed for water is now imperiling them. Only remnants survive of the Shawnee, Delaware, Flatheads, and Mandan.

The Pueblo Indians, settled and generally peaceful farmers, were no threat to the white man who had neither the wish nor the persistence to make a living on the mesas and desert.

Being peaceful farmers was no guarantee of security for Indians with good land. The Five Civilized Tribes of the East were usually better educated and governed than the whites who drove them out. There was not the slightest justification for their removal to Oklahoma. Once there, they fought to keep their tribal identities and thrived in general till the Civil War gave the government an excuse to take away more rights and land. Still, because the Five Tribes lived much the same way as white men and could do well when left alone, they have found a place in America much more easily than most other Indians.

Some good jokes—all too few—have been played when land thought worthless and allotted to Indians has produced wealth, like much Osage oil country in Oklahoma or the acreage around Palm Springs which has brought the tiny Agua Caliente band vast sums.

Very different has been the fate of the Plains Indians whose roving, buffalo-based way of life demanded vast expanses of coveted grassland. The only respectable aim of any Plains male was to be a warrior and hunter. The world of the Plains Indians vanished with the buffalo. A substitute way of life has been slow in coming. Some of the poorest Indians, and those most separated from prevailing ways of life in America, are descendants of the fiercest warriors and greatest horsemen, the Cheyenne and the Sioux.

Life expectancy in some tribes is only forty-five years. Indians have the lowest income per person of any U.S. ethnic group. Alcoholism is the leading cause of death and the horror of babies born with fetal alcohol syndrome increases every day. On some reservations, it's estimated that half the babies come into the world with this permanent brain damage, and many are born of mothers who are themselves victims of the syndrome.

Fetal alcohol syndrome is the principal cause, nation-wide, of mental retardation. Recent studies indicate that there is no safe level of drinking for a pregnant woman since alcohol has a devastating effect on the brain and organs of the developing fetus. Apart from being cursed with this lifelong handicap, most children with the syndrome are not properly cared for or educated to the limit of their abilities. This adds to the cycle of despair and wasted lives.

Tribal leaders are demanding a rehaul of the unwieldy, corruption-riddled Bureau of Indian Affairs which for 167 years had been in charge of everything from reservation law enforcement to schools. For decades, children were forcibly shipped off to BIA-run boarding schools where they were given Anglo names and forbidden to speak their own languages. At this critical stage in their lives, they were exposed to an alien culture and denied their own. Today, only about one-tenth of Indian children, 40,000 of them, attend the BIA's 180 schools.

The record is dismal. Though an Office of Indian Education was set up in 1978 and charged to ensure quality education for students, a 1991 audit by the Inspector General's Office of the Interior Department showed severe deficiencies that contributed to failing test scores on national tests for many Indian students. In addition, many schools are in shamefully poor condition.

The hopeful thing is that Native Americans themselves are urging BIA reform and taking control of their own affairs. There are now seven hundred Native American lawyers in the country. John Echo-hawk, director of the Native American Rights Fund, says there has been more litigation for Indian rights in the last twenty years than in the entire two hundred years before that.

The Smithsonian Institution agreed in 1990 to go through its collection of 18,500 Indian remains. Those identifiable as belonging to a certain tribe will be returned for burial. Other museums are following this example.

In spite of all this, the Indians have survived. In 1900 their population had dropped to about 250,000. Now it is over 700,000, about what it probably was at the coming of white men. In spite of decimation and humiliation, Indians have retained emotional and spiritual strengths vested in tribe, clan and society, which are often envied by whites who feel rootless and alone in the modern world.

Let us, all survivors in one way or another, try to understand and strengthen each other.

THE COMANCHE

Inside the Fence

Old Comanche legends said there had been no buffalo till a hero risked his life to open their cavern in the ground and stampede them out on the plains. After that the Comanche had plenty of meat.

Buffalo supplied many necessities. The hide made tepees, clothing, robes, saddles, bridles, storage bags and tough thongs. Hair could be braided into excellent ropes. Bowstrings and thread came from sinew, and cups, spoons and ornaments were fashioned from hooves, horn and bones. Buffalo chips made a strong, steady fire out on treeless prairies. All edible parts were eaten, except for the heart, which was left to make sure more buffalo would always come.

There was often a buffalo skull by the sweat lodge where men were purified of sickness or wrongdoing, and when a Comanche offered ceremonial smoke to the four directions, he might also send a puff from his pipe toward one of the guardian skulls around the camp.

11

As the buffalo spoke to Earth, the mother of all living things, by pawing the turf or loosening it with its horn, so did the Indian gain her attention by praying to her or painting himself with her clays. For years the Comanche did not believe white men could change this way of living.

But vast drifting herds of buffalo do not go with farms, towns, railroads or fences any better than do roving Indians. General William Tecumseh Sherman, who was in command of most U.S. frontier forces after the Civil War, called buffalo the Indian's "commissary" or supply center. He said that until the buffalo were gone, nothing would tame or settle the Plains tribes.

Even with Sherman bent on their destruction, enough buffalo might have lived to feed the Comanche and ease their first years on reservations. Apart from food, hunting gave braves an exciting occupation, which would have greatly helped when raiding and war parties had to stop. In 1871 huge herds still carpeted the plains in spite of sportsmen, hunters for railroad teams, and commercial butchers.

Some hides were used for robes, gloves and coats but were too soft for most uses, so the slow laborious tanning was left to Indians. Then in 1871, a tannery found how to process buffalo hides into leather that could be used for almost everything. This tannery ordered three thousand hides, offering $3.50 apiece, and the big slaughter was on.

In 1872, when the first passenger train chugged toward Dodge City, Kansas, which became the hide market and outfitting center, it was stopped by a herd three miles long and two miles wide. Some pas-

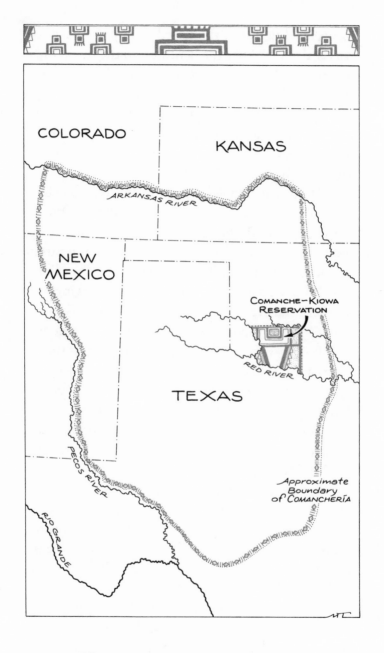

Map 1 Comanche Country

sengers whiled away the forced halt by firing into the massed bison. After the herd cleared the track, the train moved on, but it left 500 buffalo dead or dying behind, killed for no purpose except "sport."

It was this kind of senseless slaughter that maddened the Indians, especially when the herds quickly began to dwindle under the withering fire of hundreds of Sharp 50-caliber rifles.

Hordes of men went into the hide business in 1872-73. To make a fortune in skins, all that was needed was a rifle, plenty of ammunition, and a wagon and team to haul the hides. This was tempting to those who had lost homes or possessions in the Civil War, farmers who couldn't scratch a living from the soil, and everyone who just wanted to make money fast without spending much on equipment.

Buffalo were placid. If a hunter picked off the alert animals first, he might go on shooting as many as a hundred before even moving to another spot. Unpracticed hunters and skinners probably ruined three hides for each one they got to market, but the supply was still so great that prices fell to a dollar for a prime bull hide in 1874.

Instead of putting up their guns, the hunters' answer was to kill more buffalo, earning from the hides of two or three what they used to get from one. Kansas was almost bare of the massive herds, and the hide men began to gaze longingly at Indian Territory and the Staked Plains of Texas.

Some of them went to talk to the commander at Fort Dodge, hinting that they would like to go hunting on Indian lands. This commander, like General Sherman, believed the only way to stop Indian wars was to get rid of the buffalo so that the Indians would be starved onto reservations. He told the hunters that if he were in their place, he would go where the buffalo were.

So in the spring of 1874 a caravan of hide men and traders left Dodge City for the Texas Panhandle with its Staked Plains—lands closed to them by solemn treaties—treaties the Army did not intend to enforce.

The last of these treaties had been signed by chiefs of the Comanche and other Plains tribes at Medicine Lodge, Kansas, in 1867. The Indians promised to stop raids on the whites. In return, the government promised rations, supplies and a reservation in what is now southwestern Oklahoma, along with the right to hunt buffalo off the reservation.

The signing chiefs had no authority to speak for all their people. They had influence in their tribes, but the idea of a leader who could make others do his will was foreign to the Plains Indians. Certainly no Comanche wished to learn farming while there were buffalo! And the reservation, though good land, was only a small patch of the vast range the Comanches had wandered on for generations.

Their domain was the grassy rolling South Plains, spreading from central Kansas into Texas, stopping in the west at the mountains of New Mexico and Colorado, and in the east where trees grew too thick for the Comanche's liking. Besides buffalo, there were antelope and deer. Wild fruit and nuts grew in many places, and even out on the forbidding Staked Plains Comanche knew water holes. Through Texas and Mexico, the full September moon was known as the

Comanche Moon, for that was the month when they struck deep into Mexico for slaves, horses, mules and plunder.

There were five principal bands of Comanche: the Wasps or Honey-Eaters, Yap-Eaters, Wanderers, Buffalo-Eaters, and Antelope or Quohada, each having a fairly definite range, though any Comanche could live with other groups or travel freely among them. Though the Comanche had great pride in their tribe and called themselves The People, they had no tribal council, lacked the strong warrior societies of most Plains Indians, and only came together in common cause in the last summer of their freedom, at the same time the hide outfit from Dodge City was pushing into their hunting grounds.

The Comanche had seen what became of Indians who settled on reservations and tried to learn white ways. They sickened, grew poorer, starved on miserable rations, and lost their pride. It was plain to the Comanche that they would be engulfed by whites unless they did something to stop the rush of settlers and halt the slaughter of buffalo.

In 1873 a young Comanche medicine man named Isatai prophesied that the comet the Indians were watching with fear and wonder would disappear in five days and be followed by a summer-long drought.

This happened. Warriors began to listen closely to Isatai. Some swore they saw him go up to the sun to talk with the Great Spirit. Others said he had brought dead back from the spirit world. Bullets could not harm him. He belched out a wagonload of cartridges and swallowed them again. His tribesmen

16

believed him when he said the spirits had given him stronger medicine than any Indian had ever before possessed, medicine power that would defeat the whites and drive them from the Indian range.

In early summer of 1874, while the hide hunters and traders were establishing their headquarters at an old ruined post called Adobe Walls on the Staked Plains, Isatai sent messengers to all the Comanche bands.

They must join in a great Sun Dance on the fork of the Red River. There they would make medicine revealed to Isatai by the Great Spirit. The five bands, with their allies, the Kiowa, Arapaho, and Cheyenne, would join in one great force. They would attack the whites and sweep them forever from the plains.

All Comanche groups came, though the Wasps, who lived to the east near white settlers, did not like the war talk and went home. The other bands eagerly prepared for the Sun Dance.

Though the Comanche had never held a Sun Dance, they had often watched those of the Kiowa and Cheyenne, so they knew how to do it. They did not have Sun Dance dolls or Sun Dance priests, and they did not use the Cheyenne rites of self-torture, driving skewers through their chest muscles. But they put up the traditional lodge in the ceremonial way and mounted a stuffed buffalo on the center pole. The Comanche had also watched dances in the New Mexican pueblos and from these borrowed mud-daubed clowns who charged through the camp, swatting people and making everybody laugh.

On the fourth day of the lodge building, warriors made mock battle on a circular enclosure symbolizing Adobe Walls. They knew about the hide hunters and meant them to be their first target in the campaign that would rid the plains of whites.

After the sham fight, a crier went through the camp, calling people out of their lodges. They moved toward the dance lodge in the middle of the great camp circle, each band singing and doing its favorite dance. When they met before the lodge, the Comanche danced together, all the nations except the Wasps, for the first—and last—time. They went to sleep exhausted, glad and confident. It was good to be together like this, to see how many they were, and how strong!

On the fifth day the Sun Dancers filed into the lodge, painted themselves, and danced to the drums, blowing their eagle bone whistles. They danced late that night and for the next three days, going without food and water, though they could rest on beds of sage spread for them in the lodge. Some had visions and worked miracles, but this great dance was not for individual power. It was to make them strong together, give them the power Isatai had promised.

When the dance was over, the warriors started for Adobe Walls. Isatai told them it would fall without an Indian death. They attacked early one morning in late June.

Isatai was naked except for a cap of sage stems. All the horses were painted with magic color that would turn away bullets. The Indians had great faith in their medicine. But when the whites, who had been warned by some other Indians, opened fire with their long-range buffalo rifles, the war party fell back, furious and baffled.

———

What was wrong? They had done what Isatai had told them.

They fought on, killing three whites caught outside the protecting walls; but the hunters inside the post could pick off warriors who rode close, so nine braves were killed and more wounded, among them one of the bravest young chiefs, Quanah Parker. Isatai's painted horse was killed under him.

He had no power. There was no medicine. He had deceived his people! One chief whose son had been killed wanted to flog Isatai, but friends held him back. To be so disgraced was punishment enough. No one, ever again, would look up to Isatai or follow him.

It was not losing men or the battle that plunged the Comanche into despair. They were used to fights, victory and defeat. What crushed their will to fight at Adobe Walls was the realization that the Great Spirit was not helping them, that magic paint and Sun Dances were no good against long-range rifles.

The warriors drifted away from the hide hunters' post, rejoining their women and children in small bands that roamed the drought-stricken prairies through that summer, raiding whites when they could, knowing their free days were numbered, but determined to stay out as long as they could. Perhaps sometimes they passed Adobe Walls, deserted by the alarmed hide hunters, and saw the Indian skulls displayed on poles.

It was the driest, hottest summer in years. Grasshoppers flew in dark clouds, settling where they found anything green. They gnawed trees and shrubs to the bark, devoured grass to its roots, left the plains barren and hungry. Creeks and springs that usually flowed all summer went dry except for an occasional hole. When the summer was a time of near-starvation, what would the winter be?

Even before Adobe Walls, many Kiowa under their great chief Kicking Bird, many Cheyenne, and some Comanche had settled on the Fort Sill reservation. Through the summer more drifted in, especially as the drought lengthened and military preparations were seen for an operation that would close in around the Indians still on the prairies and force them into Fort Sill. General Philip Sheridan meant to defeat and humble the swift-riding Comanche as thoroughly as he had beaten the South in the Civil War.

During summer and fall the soldiers made ready. Ammunition, rations, and grain were collected, horses shod, guns inspected, wagon wheels greased, and saddles oiled. Once the soldiers started, they would unrelentingly keep after the Indians, giving them no time to hunt, rest, or let their horses graze. Troops would close in on the Indians from all directions.

From Indian Territory, troops would move from Fort Sill and Camp Supply; up from Forts Griffin and Concho in Texas; from Fort Union in New Mexico. There would be no escape this time.

After a few early skirmishes the Quohada Comanche managed to refuge in the high Staked Plains. The whites did not know where the scarce water holes were and could not stay on those steppes long enough to drive the Indians in. If next summer the Quohada were still out, then all the forces of the Army could go after them. Meanwhile, after brushes with the converging three thousand U.S. soldiers, the remaining Comanche, with their Kiowa and Cheyenne allies, were either going into Fort Sill or taking cover deep in Palo Duro Canyon.

Southeast of what is now Amarillo, Texas, Palo Duro Canyon is a great rift more than 40 miles long, almost 1,000 feet deep in places, and 6 miles or so wide. It had always been a favorite winter camp of Plains Indians. Sheltered from the worst storms, watered by a fork of the Red River, with good grass and plenty of trees, the Indians hoped to endure the time of blizzards.

Who could tell what might happen to them by summer? Perhaps the whites, in their strange fashion, might fall again to battling each other. Or the buffalo might multiply. Or perhaps a great leader would rise up to gather the remaining free Indians in a force that would stop the hunters and settlers.

What happened was that Colonel Ranald Mac-Kenzie, who had in the past defeated even the tough Quohada and who was an expert Indian trailer and fighter, discovered their camp. Late in September his scouts gazed down through the mist-hazed cedars and saw hundreds of tepees scattered for miles up and down the canyon. They hurried back to tell Mac-Kenzie. A few days later, as day was breaking, the regiment came to the canyon rim and searched for a way down.

Silhouetted against the dawn, the troopers would have been easily seen by a guard, but the Indians had posted none. At last, the soldiers found a narrow goat path zigzagging downward. Leading their mounts, the men slipped and slid single file down the canyon. They would have been sure targets during this hazardous approach, but three companies reached the canyon bottom before the Indians roused.

The troops galloped down the canyon while the Indians, startled from sleep, peered out of their lodges and saw charging soldiers. Some warriors seized their weapons and fought, but many usually valiant men, caught without time to prepare or paint for battle, fled with the women and children up the northwest side of the canyon, leaving behind all their belongings, except what could be snatched up and run with.

The defending Indians took cover among the cedars and rocks on the sides of the canyon, but some troopers kept them pinned down with long-range carbine fire while other soldiers captured the thousands of horses and mules abandoned by the Indians.

Mackenzie was not interested in killing the fugitives. If their camp and animals were gone, they would have to surrender. Instead of worrying about the escaping people, the soldiers heaped up tepees, lodge poles, saddles, robes, clothing, dried meat, weapons—everthing that would burn—and set them on fire. They knocked holes in cooking kettles and ruined all the Indians' necessities.

Mackenzie finished this destruction by midafternoon and withdrew, driving the Indians' horses and mules, while several companies covered the removal.

Once back on the plateau, Mackenzie placed his regiment in a guarding square around the captured animals and rejoined his supply train. Next morning he commanded that the 1,400 horses and mules be shot, except for 336 which he gave to the Tonkawa scouts. Only by leaving them on foot and without shelter or food could the Comanche really be conquered.

The night of the disaster was made even worse for the Indians by a hard rain. No one had a tepee. Those who had packs slept on them. Everyone was hungry. Only one warrior had been killed, but loss of their horses and supplies was more crippling than the death of many braves.

The Indians scattered, but though some stayed out on the plains awhile or refuged with other bands, the region swarmed with troopers. Starving, most of them destitute, the once-proud Comanche were forced to surrender and go into Fort Sill.

Even bands still owning horses knew they could not elude the soldiers who swept the plains. There were fourteen real battles during that final hounding of the Kiowa, Comanche and Southern Cheyenne, but more than by fighting, the Indians were beaten by being constantly chased, never being able to hunt or rest.

As they straggled or were driven into Fort Sill, each band was put in the great stone horse corral. Horses, mules and weapons were taken from them. Saddles, robes and household goods were also taken and shut in a warehouse. The Indians never got any of this back, and no one knows what happened to it.

The most warlike men were locked in the basement of the guardhouse. More than a hundred other warriors were caged in an unfinished icehouse that had no roof. These men were given pup tents, and once a day an Army wagon pulled alongside while soldiers tossed hunks of raw meat over the walls as if they were feeding wild animals.

Women and children were put in prison camps along Cache Creek east of the post. Gradually, the men were allowed there, too, except for the most feared warriors, who were going to be sent into exile in Florida so that they would not stir their people up to fresh fighting when spring, with its greening grass, would call Indians to try for freedom.

The Indians' horses and mules were taken west of the post and shot; but by the time 750 rotting carcasses brought a sickening stench the commander decided to auction off the rest of the herds, except for several hundred he gave to scouts. The Indians lost about 7,500 head of stock, worth perhaps $250,000. The auctions brought in only about $22,000, but at least this was credited to the bands who had given them up and would later be used to purchase for them sheep, which they didn't want, and some cattle.

Disease and hunger deepened the sadness of the Indians that winter of defeat. Still, those camping on the flats outside the post were lucky compared with some Kiowa who were shut up all winter in the stone corral.

There was no room for tents. A roof projecting from the walls provided shelter for mares and colts, and this was where the Indians camped. To see the sky, they looked up through the open center of the corral or peered through windows cut high in the walls.

Cattle were driven in for butchering. There was no space for drying meat or proper fires to cook it, so usually the stringy tough meat was eaten raw. It was too hard for some old people to chew, and children cried for buffalo meat.

The Indians had no way to wash or make new clothing. Butchering in the center of the corral made the whole place smell bad. Many became physically ill as well as heartsick.

Worst of all, there was nothing for the people to do. Some women saved hides from the slaughtered cows and worked with heartbreaking patience to tan them without enough tallow and brain to make the proper mixture. Only the bravest women persisted till they made stiff cowhide clothes for themselves so that babies could have their soft buckskins.

Many children died that winter, but others were born. At last the captives could glimpse budding green along the creek, delicate bursts of purple and white blossoms. And then they heard a meadowlark and believed that they would live.

A little later, the last Kiowa surrendered, and the people in the corral were allowed to go camp a short distance from Kicking Bird's camp.

Kicking Bird had worked for peace with the whites and had kept his band of Kiowa on the reservation during the uprisings of the last summer. Now he had the ugly task of selecting which prisoners should be sent to Fort Marion in Florida. Seventy-four of the most dangerous and hostile Comanche, Cheyenne and Kiowa were to be held there till their tribes were past all thought of rebellion. Kicking Bird was no traitor to his people, but he knew that continued fighting could only bring destruction to them.

He visited the warriors who were going to Florida, and told them good-bye and that he would work for their return to their own people.

Maman-ti, the Owl Prophet, who had been one of the last Kiowa raiders to surrender, stared at Kicking Bird and spoke slowly with hatred. "You think you have done well, Kicking Bird! You remain free, a big man with the whites. But you will not live long."

On the prison train to Florida, Maman-ti put a curse on Kicking Bird and promised the other dejected captives that Kicking Bird would die but that his own life would be forfeited for killing a fellow Kiowa. Maman-ti fell ill and died a few days after reaching Florida. Kicking Bird was only forty and in good health, but he bacame unexpectedly ill and died on May 4, 1875, after sending for his friend, Agent James Haworth and giving him a fine gray horse. "Tell my people to keep in the good road," Kicking Bird said. "I am dying holding fast the white man's hand."

Now that the war leaders were imprisoned far away in Florida, the Indians on the reservation were allowed to range freely and even hunt outside its boundaries as long as they caused no trouble.

The only sizable band left at large was the Quohada, far out on the Staked Plains. Colonel MacKenzie sent word to their principal chief, Quanah Parker, that the Quohada could live in peace on the reservation, but if they did not come in speedily, troopers would hunt them down and kill them all.

Quanah, the famed son of a white Texas woman captive, had fought MacKenzie before and knew he meant his warning. There was no chance of surviving another season. In June, Quanah brought his band into Fort Sill, 100 warriors and about 300 women and children. They gave up their weapons, and their 1,400 ponies were sold at auction.

So ended the free days on the plains. Now the Indians and the Whites in charge of them had to find a way for them to live.

Under the disdained 1867 Treaty of Medicine Lodge, the Indians were to be given seeds and farming implements so that they could grow food instead of hunting it. Little notice was taken of the fact that the plains tribes scorned farming and had never stayed in one place long enough to grow a crop.

The Indians were also given thoroughly unsuitable clothing. Once their buffalo hides and buckskins were gone, they made vests out of coats, made leggings out of hose and trousers, and wrapped up in the calico instead of sewing it into dresses.

Buffalo were all but extinct and game was scarce, but still the Indians were expected to hunt and farm for much of their food. Supplemental rations were beef, cornmeal, sugar, salt, coffee, soap, with additions or substitutions of bacon, beans, salt pork, flour, hominy and rice. Often even the meager rations were not furnished, and hunger was almost a constant state for many Indians over a period of years.

They were used to a diet mostly of meat and did not like any of the rations except coffee and sugar. Cornmeal they despised to the point of sometimes feeding it to their horses.

Agents and military commanders experimented with different ways of teaching the Indians "how to walk the white man's road," a path none of them liked, though defeat and the passing of the buffalo left them no choice.

Houses were built for ten friendly chiefs, but most of them preferred to camp in the yards and let their dogs occupy the houses. The children had fun running through the empty rooms and making them echo. One little boy remembered how he asked his mother to make his bed in the fireplace so that he could look up the chimney to the stars.

Colonel Ranald MacKenzie had pursued the Indians till they had surrendered, but he wanted to help them settle into living with hope, comfort, and self-respect. With money from their auctioned horses and mules, he bought sheep and goats in New Mexico and had them brought to the reservation. He reasoned that these animals could supply the Comanche with meat and wool. They could learn to make rugs like the Navajo and soon be self-supporting.

In common with most schemes for helping Indians, this one ignored Plains Indian tradition and aptitudes. Plains Indians had always looked down on peoples who kept sheep and goats and raided them at every oppportunity. Neither did they like mutton or goat flesh.

Many of the animals died on the way to Oklahoma or in that first winter. Colonel MacKenzie had them held till spring of 1876. Then he called together all the Indians, who put on their best clothes and came to the distrubution as if going to a party.

Each band was given a small herd. They were told how good the meat was, what good clothes could be made of wool, and how they could make and sell blankets.

No Comanche knew how to weave, and none of them cared to learn. Imagine how you would feel if, suddenly, all of your regular food and clothing disappeared and a Comanche showed you a buffalo, told you how to slaughter, skin and use it, how to make tepees and robes, and eat the liver with a little gall squeezed on it. These things would still be very hard for you, you would get very discouraged while trying, and you would want your accustomed food, shelter and clothes.

As soon as the Comanche got their flocks home, they ignored them or chased them out on the prairie and shot them with arrows. A few escaped to fall to coyotes. The experiment was a total waste.

MacKenzie had also bought some cattle for the Indians. It is a shame he didn't spend all the auction money on cows, for the Comanche and Kiowa liked them and enjoyed taking care of them. Cattle were more like buffalo, and handling and raising them was interesting work, man's work, which was above all what these Indians needed at that time when war was barred to them and hunting brought in little food.

Unfortunately, rations fell short so often that most of the Indians' stock had to be killed and eaten before it could breed more cattle. Even when allowed to hunt off the reservation, the Indians could find almost no game, but they still went, for it was the most cherished part of their old life permitted to them now.

In 1878 the agent let them set off for their old hunting grounds. They went in high spirits, eager for the buffalo who would feed and clothe them.

They found only bones bleached white by the sun, sometimes in piles where the hide hunters had skinned hundreds at a time. Scouts hunted up and down the creeks and buffalo wallows. Somewhere there must be a herd left! Perhaps the buffalo were in the north and would come south when the frosts began.

Other game was pitifully scarce. The hunters could barely live on the few antelope they found. Winter was coming. The time the agent had allowed them for the hunt was over. Not a single buffalo had been glimpsed.

Some of the hunters gave up and went back to Fort Sill. Others stayed out, hoping that bad weather would drive the buffalo south. They were caught starving in the winter's first snowstorm and had to kill some of their ponies for food. The agent sent a messenger to take them food and bring them back to the reservation. They came sadly.

The buffalo were truly gone. For Indians there would never again be buffalo meat drying on racks for winter food, robes for warmth, or delicious morsels of tongue and hump. Even the bones would not stay long on the prairies, for men would collect them to sell for fertilizer and buttons.

Not even the grass was the same. Instead of the waving buffalo grass that changed its colors like ruffled velvet as the sun and wind struck it, there was a tough-rooted short new kind of grass that was dull and had no sheen.

After that last starving hunt, the Comanche bands broke up. Some war chiefs resigned. Most of the Indian stopped living in villages and settled on farms with their families or close relatives. Some got cattle and raised them with success, but the Indian agents kept trying to make crop planters and garden growers of them.

Apart from a dislike of what he called women's work, farming went against the Plains Indian's idea of the earth as his mother. Should he cut off her hair, the grass? Should he break her bones, the rocks? If he cut her with plows and hoes, would she receive him back to her when he died?

The Comanche were as strange to the plow as were their fleet little ponies and resisted it as much.

One agent hit on the idea of placing ropes on the ground as guidelines between which the furrow should be made. But after a field was plowed and planted and when it came time to thin out the weaker plants so that the others would grow better, no Indian liked to do this, for it seemed a waste of the crop he had grown with such toil.

Through this bitter time of change and struggle, Quanah Parker was an example and encouragement to his people. Shortly after his surrender in the summer of 1875, he had visited the Mescalero Apache, watched their religious use of peyote, and decided that this might help the Comanche through this period, when old ways were shattered and new ones hard to find.

Peyote is a small spineless cactus that has been used for centuries in Mexico for religious ceremonies. Chewing enough of the buds can bring visions or at least alter perception so that one has new eyes and ears—"sees sound" and "hears color." The Comanche took the peyote as some churches take communion, solemnly and with a mystic sense of union. They came in from their scattered farms to sit together, sing, and share peyote and their visions. This gave them a spiritual comfort that sustained them through early reservation days. Peyote is still used in the Native American Church as a rite of fellowship and enlightenment. Organized in 1918, this church has members in nearly all tribes and is the largest cohesive Indian group in the United States.

Ration days became gala occasions with feasting, horse racing and gambling. When beef cattle were issued, the men and boys chased them as if they were buffalo till they were brought down. Often, with friends and relations close by to visit, it was tempting to have a grand holiday and eat all the week's or two weeks' rations while gathered at the agency. Once most Indians were raising cattle and crops, a few would journey in to pick up rations for their neighborhood, and after 1901, only Indians who could not work were given rations.

Agent P. B. Hunt organized the first Indian police in 1878. They could accomplish more among their people than could white officers, and they settled many problems that would have led to serious trouble had whites intervened. Most of their work, though, was turning back Texas cattle whose owners wanted the Indians' grazing land and were happy to pay dollar-per-head trespass fine that U.S. troopers helped the Indian Police collect.

Many cattlemen considered the fines grass rental. There was no real way to keep them off the reservation, so Agent Hunt tried to turn the situation to the Indians' advantage. In 1881 drought brought a dangerous crop shortage. Rations were never enough, and at times like this the Indians were nearly starving. Hunt told the cattlemen they could graze their herds on reservation land and pay in beef to feed the Indians.

Hunt got into trouble with Washington for this, but at least the Indians ate better. By 1885 the Bureau of Indian Affairs decided that since the cattle could not keep off this "Big Pasture," legal arrangements should be made to be sure the Indians at least got paid for their grass. Grazing leases were arranged, and these sums contributed a large amount to tribal funds.

Dealing with the big trail drives from Texas to Kansas was more of a problem, but the cowboys usually gave the Indians some cattle, and Comanche and Kiowa herds were often increased by little calves too young to travel when their mothers were driven on.

The Indians did not like to use the white men's courts, so Agent Hunt helped begin an Indian Court which tried reservation cases from 1886 till 1901, when the reservation was done away with. Quanah Parker was one of the judges who helped settle many problems according to Indian ideas of right.

Some Kiowa served as scouts for the Army at Fort Sill, but not many Comanche enlisted. Quanah used his influence against it, as he did when an Indian cavalry troop was formed in 1892. Quanah argued that white missionaries taught Indians that war was wrong. Why, then, did the whites urge Indians to fight?

Once the Comanche saw with their own eyes that the buffalo were gone, they did not hope for a return to the happy old life. Under Quanah's leadership, they raised livestock and did some farming, sent their children to school, and hoped for the future.

If Kicking Bird had not died, he probably would have had a similar influence on the Kiowa. But without a strong leader to help them get used to the white man's world, the Kiowa believed several prophets who announced that they had power to rid the land of whites and bring back the buffalo. Each quickly failed, but the Kiowa kept hoping for a miracle.

The Kiowa had another strong reason for resisting the whites. The Sun Dance had long been their most important social and religious gathering. They had special dolls and priests for it and longed to go on holding it in early summer.

Their agent was against it. He said it came just at the time when their crops needed care. The missionaries hated and feared what they called a pagan festival. In 1889 the Kiowa were forcibily prevented from giving one, and their discontent grew even worse.

They were more than ready to listen when, in 1890, word of a new Messiah ran like wildfire through the Indian tribes. This Messiah had already appeared to the white men, but they had killed him. This time He was coming to the Indians!

He would bring a new earth. Vast herds of buffalo and sleek fast ponies would graze on changing seas of grass watered by streams and rivers that never went dry. No railroads or telegraphs or fences or farms would mar the countryside and block off trails.

It would be as it had been before, only better, for all the dead would live again and there would be no more sickness, death or war. The white man would disappear with the old world he had devastated, but the Indians were not to fight or kill him. All they needed to do was pray and hold the Ghost Dance until the Messiah came.

Wovoka, a Paiute Indian of Nevada, was the Ghost Dance prophet, and some thought him to be the Messiah. The joyful vision swept across the plains, north to the Sioux and Northern Cheyenne, Shoshone, Ute, Pawnee, Crow and south to the Southern Cheyenne, Arapaho, Kiowa and Comanche. Navajo, Apache and Pueblo tribes in New Mexico were not attracted by it, nor were the Eastern Indians of the Five Civilized Tribes, whose land in Indian Territory adjoined the Kiowa-Comanche reservation.

Mainly the Ghost Dance was done by those peoples whose way of life had been completely shattered by the white men and who were not finding conditions more hopeful or tolerable in 1890 than they had been in 1875.

The Comanche took almost no part in the Dance. Many of the warriors remembered Isatai with his great false medicine and promises, and Quanah did all he could to keep his people aloof. Besides, they had the unifying ritual of peyote that gave them a feeling of belonging to the earth and each other in spite of all changes.

Of the Comanche, only the Wasp band, the single group that had left the Sun Dance before Adobe Walls, joined the Ghost Dance.

The Kiowa took to it eagerly, as did the Southern Cheyenne, their neighbors. An Arapaho medicine man named Sitting Bull (no relation to the Sioux chief who fought Custer) brought the dance with its prophecies to the southern plains. It was lucky that the Army commander at Fort Sill kept an eye on the dancing but did not try to stop it, even when nervous whites tried to make him halt it.

During the dance people fell into trances. Sometimes they had visions of their beloved dead and the wonderful new world their prophet would bring. Some educated people today spend much effort and money trying to speak with their dead. It is no marvel that Indians whose belief in the supernatural touched every phase of their lives should embrace a faith that promised them heaven on earth and reunion with their loved ones.

There were many Ghost Dance dreams. Perhaps the one with the strangest result was that of a Cheyenne woman who told the dance leaders she had seen a fine new bed.

The leaders felt this was an invitation to make a bed for the Messiah. When He had come to the white men, He had no home and was only given a place with the cattle. Indians would not treat Him like that. They knew how it felt to be homeless. For their Messiah they would make a lodge and place a good bed in it, the best they could find.

They were very poor, but they got enough money together to buy a beautiful bed of white iron, with four brass balls on its posts, a mattress and bright blankets. There were no buffalo robes to make a good lodge, but they put a canvas tent around the bed and waited. They had danced, they had got the bed, they had prayed for their leader.

Now He would come.

But He did not. They watched Coyote Butte, where they had set up the tent and bed, but no matter how long they danced and called to Him and the spirits, nothing happened.

Most of the people still hoped and believed, but at last they sent a young man named Apaitan to find the prophet Wovoka and ask him when the Messiah would come. Apaitan had been a strong believer in the dance, for he had lost his small son whom he loved very much and hoped to see him again in the new world when the dead came back to life.

Apaitan journeyed among the Sioux and Bannock and at last found Wovoka in Nevada on the Paiute reservation. Wovoka was alarmed at the excitement his visions had brought. No, he told Apaitan. He, Wovoka, was not the Messiah. His message had been exaggerated. There would be no new world. The dead would not rise, nor would the buffalo return. The tribes must stop the dance. There was no hope nor power in it.

Sadly Apaitan took this back to the reservation. All those who had believed gathered to hear him. Kiowa, Caddo, Cheyenne, Wichita, Arapaho and a few Comanche listened with sinking hearts as his words crushed their desperate faith.

A few refused to accept Apaitan's words and kept on dancing, but when spring came—the time when the Messiah was generally expected—and then summer and autumn, even the staunchest followers realized that the Ghost Dance could not bring back the world that had vanished.

So the faith died in Indian Territory, but there was no bloodshed like the terrible slaughter of Wounded Knee which resulted from the Army's fear of the Sioux dancers. Among the Southern Plains tribes, those who were unreconciled waited for death, but most people gave up any mystical dreams and tried to make the best of this world the white man had forced on them.

The land greed of the westward-pushing whites made this even harder than it had to be. The Comanche and Kiowa who had once roamed all the South Plains now lived in a corner of Indian Terrri-tory, later to become Oklahoma, which was also home to the Southern Cheyenne, Caddo, Wichita, the Five Civilized Tribes, and surviving small tribes squeezed gradually out of their eastern or northern homes. Even the remnant of their former land, which was the reservation, was not to be left to the Comanche and Kiowa.

By 1890 land-hungry settlers were eyeing the miles of good graze which these tribes leased to cattlemen for pasture. Over bitter protests from Indians and cattlemen, the Jerome Agreement was made at Fort Sill in 1892.

Each man, woman and child of the Comanche and Kiowa tribes was to have 160 acres of land. Two sections of each township would be used for school purposes, and two more were for public institutions and welfare. Four tracts would be held for the Indians' collective use; the largest of these was the "Big Pasture" of 414,720 acres, which bordered the Red River. In payment for their other lands, the Indians were to be paid $2,000,000.

When the Indians learned the terms of the agreement most of them were furious. They accused their Kiowa interpreter of not telling them what was really being said and of telling the commissioners that the tribes agreed to the conditions they knew nothing about.

Some of the angriest Indians made medicine to kill the interpreter. They threw mud at a doll which represented him. The interpreter died on his way home from the council, and the white commissioners also died within a short time.

The Indians continued to protest the agreement arguing that it was not legal since many tribesmen had not been at the council and those who were had been betrayed. Cattlemen who needed to keep their grazing leases also lobbied in Washington to prevent the agreement's ratification, but in 1900 it became law.

There was nothing the Indians could do but select their land. That not chosen by them was surveyed into 160-acre homesteads and opened by lottery. Within weeks, that last small corner the Plains Indians had believed would at least be theirs swarmed with homesteaders building, planting, and starting towns.

But as long as there was common Indian land, the whites would covet it, especially the more than 400,000 acres of the "Big Pasture." Pressure was brought on Congress. In 1906 each of the 517 children born since the first allotments were chosen was given 160 acres and the rest of the land was sold. Next year, in 1907, Oklahoma became a state.

Since then the Comanche and Kiowa have lived, on farms or in small towns in southwestern Oklahoma, some prospering, some not doing so well. Stock raising is a favored occupation. Some Kiowa have become wealthy from the discovery of oil on their land.

Though their early days on the reservation were full of sickness, despair and hunger, the Kiowa and Comanche now live as well as their white neighbors. There are a number of well-known Kiowa artists, and Indians from both tribes are found in business and professional life.

Only a few very old people remember the days before they came "inside the fence."

FURTHER SUGGESTED READING

Andrist, Ralph, *The Long Death*. New York, Macmillian, 1965.

Brown, Dee, *Bury My Heart At Wounded Knee*. New York, Holt, Rinehart & Winston, 1970.

Fehrenbach, T. R., *The Comanches*. New York, Knopf, 1984.

Josephy Jr., Alvin M., *Now That the Buffalo's Gone*. Norman, University of Oklahoma Press, 1984.

Marriot, Alice, *The Ten Grandmothers*. Norman, University of Oklahoma Press, 1945.

Momaday, M. Scott, *The Way To Rainy Mountain*. Albuquerque, University of New Mexico Press, 1976.

Nye, W. S., *Carbine and Lance*. Norman, University of Oklahoma Press, 1937.

Wellman, Paul I., *Death on the Prairies; The Thirty Years' Struggle for the Western Plains*. Lincoln, University of Nebraska Press, 1987.

Wright, Muriel, *Guide to the Indian Tribes of Oklahoma*. Norman, University of Oklahoma Press, 1951.

THE CHEYENNE

Dull Knife's Homing

Long ago the Cheyenne were two different tribes who lived beyond the Missouri River in the region of many lakes. Once when food grew scarce, a young hero called Standing on the Ground gave one tribe buffalo, corn and the sacred buffalo hat that would preserve the herds so that the people need never starve.

Sweet Medicine, a hero of the other tribe, showed them how to make arrows to kill game and gave them four sacred arrows, which would keep the people safe and aid them in battle. These were kept in a piece of hide cut from the back of a coyote, and special ceremonies had to be performed when their powers were needed.

In the spring Sweet Medicine was young, but he grew old with the winter and repeated this cycle for many normal lifetimes. When he felt he had lived enough, he called the Cheyenne together.

They would go west, he told them, and there they would find a strange kind of buffalo with a tail

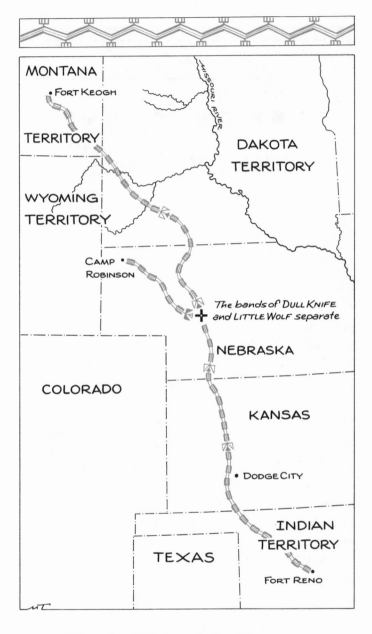

Map 2 Flight of the Cheyenne

reaching far down in back and hooves that were not split in the middle. They would ride this creature and he would carry them in war and the hunt.

All would be well with them for a long time, but someday they would meet men of a whitish color with hair growing on the fronts of their faces. These men would bring death and misfortune to the Indians.

Generations after Sweet Medicine left them, the Cheyenne had moved to the plains and become great horsemen. They still had their buffalo hat, the sacred arrows, and their hero's warning, which became fatally true as whites pushed into the Great Plains.

The Cheyenne fled from early travelers such as Lewis and Clark, and they avoided contact with whites as long as possible. Though white soldiers called them "the best fighters the sun ever shone on," they did not hope to defeat Sweet Medicine's prophecy forever, but they hoped to delay it.

White men, however, were not long in living up to the worst that could be expected of them. In spite of treaties and promises, whites kept pushing into Cheyenne lands. By this time the tribe had divided into the Southern Cheyenne, who lived on the Arkansas River in what is now southern Colorado, and the Northern Cheyenne, who roamed the headwaters of the Platte and Yellowstone Rivers in present Montana, Wyoming and the Dakotas. Though the two groups often camped, fought and hunted together, the Northern division allied with the Sioux, while the Southern group often joined with Kiowa, Arapaho and Comanche in their last desperate stands against the whites.

One of the most brutal slaughters in American history happened in 1864 at Sand Creek in Colorado. White settlers and travelers lived in dread of Indian attacks, which were becoming numerous, and Colonel J.M. Chivington set out with cannon and 750 cavalrymen to punish the Cheyenne.

He did not care whether he caught the guilty. For his purpose, one Cheyenne was as good as another, and if his men killed babies, what did it matter? They would grow into troublesome warriors and have to be conquered later.

Early one morning Chivington fell upon Black Kettle's peaceful camp. Most of the Indians were children, women, and old men. Black Kettle had been friendly to the whites and had tried to keep his young men from raiding. He ran up a white flag to show the soldiers his camp was at peace, but troopers charged through the village, shooting, clubbing, bayoneting.

The few Cheyenne who could get to their weapons fought hard and killed nine soldiers. Estimates of the Indians murdered that day ran from 100 to 800, but the most likely number seems about 163. Over two-thirds of these were women and children.

Chivington and his soldiers reported a big fight against hostile warriors: "Nine hundred to a thousand warriors," he claimed and vowed his men had done nobly. They took scalps back to Denver and showed them between acts in a theatre.

But there had been some soldiers who protested the massacre and would not take part, and there were some survivors in the Cheyenne camp, one of them Robert Bent, the half-Cheyenne son of William Bent, the great trader and friend of the Indians. When the

truth of Sand Creek came out, Congress sent three of
its members to investigate the massacre.

Some of Chivington's men who had been at Sand
Creek testified against him. So did William Bent and
Kit Carson, who called Chivington and his followers
dogs and cowards.

Both of these men knew the Cheyenne well. Bent
had married a woman of the tribe. He swore that if
the government would give him power to act for it, he
could stop the depredations along the Arkansas that
had settlers living in terror. He and Kit Carson knew
it would be hard for the warrior nomads to change to
settled ways, but a number of the chiefs knew their
people must learn how to live with the white man's
civilization. These chiefs wanted seeds and farming
implements. They remember how they had once
lived from planting crops, and now that the buffalo
were becoming scarcer, they told all Cheyenne who
would listen that they should once again grow corn
and other foods. If the government had given Carson
and Bent funds and authority to work with the peace-
minded Cheyenne, much bloodshed and grief for
both white and Indians could have been avoided. But
instead of such a healing step, the government
ordered the Cheyenne to live south of the Arkansas
near the Kiowa and Comanche.

The United States did at least pay reparations in
money and land to those Cheyenne who lost relatives
at Sand Creek, and if Chivington had not retired, he
would have faced a court-martial. Regrettably, civilian law could not try him for actions while he was in
the Army, and the Army could not try a civilian. He
went back to Ohio and went into politics, but the

taint of Sand Creek fouled his name and he did not prosper.

The government had no consistent plan to help the Indians adjust to reservation life, and the reservations were not clearly defined. Rations were inadequate. For several years Cheyenne roamed the prairies like other Plains tribes. Some hotheads killed whites when they could, while the Army hunted down and killed peaceful Indians, as well as warring ones.

Both whites and Indians killed each other's women and children, scalped and mutilated the dead. The difference was that white men claimed to be civilized. Also, the whites were taking over lands solemnly vowed by treaty to the Indians, killing the buffalo without which they could not live. The Indians were defending not only their lives but a way of life, one they loved.

In 1868 the same Black Kettle whose camp had been attacked at Sand Creek and who had managed to escape with his severely wounded wife was camped with his band on the Washita River in what is now Oklahoma. In spite of Sand Creek, Black Kettle resolutely urged peace, since he knew war and raiding could only bring the Cheyenne misery and make it harder to get satisfactory terms from the government.

Some warriors mocked him for this, and in spite of it, General George Custer fell on his village one November morning and killed as many men, women and children as he could before the Indians camped down river could come to their rescue. When these warriors rushed up, Custer and his force withdrew. Along with many of his people, Black Kettle and his wife were dead.

From that time on, the Southern Cheyenne were bitter and joined with the Kiowa and Comanche in raiding, till all of them were finally forced onto the Oklahoma reservations in 1875.

Northward, the Sioux and Northern Cheyenne were angered by the gold seekers crowding into their sacred Black Hills. They played fight-and-chase with the Army till they made the mistake of whipping Custer at the Little Big Horn in late June, 1876.

Savages to triumph over seasoned U.S. cavalry? It couldn't happen—or if it did, it must be punished with such crushing, relentless power that the warriors would, once and for all, know that resistance could bring them only death and ruin. What if the land had been secured to the Indians by treaty? White men wanted it now.

Railroads must be built. Posts would be established to keep Indians under control. The mighty Sioux chief Red Cloud had settled on the reservation, and those who did not submit would be hunted down and forcibly driven in.

That summer after the Custer fight, preparations began for a relentless winter expedition. By now the Army had learned to press Indians in the cold months when it was difficult for women and children to travel, when snows made it hard to pitch tepees and find food. With other enemies, Indians had always warred in the summer; in the snows, they warred with winter itself.

Now, General Ranald MacKenzie, the same soldier who had hounded the Kiowa and Comanche into Fort Sill, gathered a force of more than 2,000 men: infantry, cavalry, artillery, Indian scouts, drivers, and packers for the mule-pulled supply wagons.

Several Sioux villages were surrounded in darkness early in the campaign and captured without fighting. These Sioux were sent to Fort Robinson in the northeast corner of Nebraska. MacKenzie pushed on toward the large Cheyenne village scouts had spotted at the head of the Crazy Woman fork of the Powder River.

This was the village of Dull Knife. He was an Old Man Chief, which meant that he was one of the four principal chiefs and had sworn to place his people's good above his own. A respected elder warrior, he had been one of the elite Dog Soldiers in his youth, but for twenty years he had worked for peace with the whites, except in 1865, when all the Cheyenne were stung to fury by Chivington's massacre. Still, MacKenzie expected battle, for some of Dull Knife's young men had been at the Custer fight.

During the November night more than a thousand cavalrymen and scouts stole up to the village. They attacked at first dawn. Dull Knife's son was killed in the first charge, but most warriors managed to snatch up rifles and ammunition. Rushing their families to cover in the rocks and bluffs behind the village, the men fought stoutly, but the overwhelming number of soldiers drove them back to the bluffs.

From there, they had to watch in helpless anger as troopers and scouts heaped together lodges, clothing, robes, weapons, the dried meat which was meant to feed the people through the winter, and even the lodge poles. The troopers set these on fire. The greasy smoke curling into the air meant ruin, for in the winter there was no way to replace the precious belongings and supplies.

Knowing that the Cheyenne were without food and shelter, the soldiers did not try to crush them in battle. Blizzards and hunger would do that. The troopers captured most of the horses and drove them away from the smoking village while Dull Knife's band, living on a few horses they had managed to save, made their sad journey to Crazy Horse's camp of the Sioux on the Tongue River. Apart from Dull Knife's son, a number of the bravest men had been killed, and there was mourning for loved ones, as well as for possessions.

The Sioux welcomed Dull Knife's cold, hungry people and gave them all the food and clothing they could, taking them into their lodges. But another command of soldiers under Colonel (later General) Nelson A. Miles picked up their trail and harried Crazy Horse's and Dull Knife's band through that winter, giving them no chance to rest or hunt. The Indians fought off the cavalry in a number of retreats, but as spring came, the Indians were nearly starving and were completely exhausted.

General George Crook, the top Commander for that region, was respected by the Indians as one white man who had a straight tongue. Crook had fought and subdued Indians throughout his career, but he understood their troubles and used all his influence to get good treatment for them. He insisted that the United States help the Indians become self-supporting.

"They are surrounded on all sides," he wrote angrily in the *Army and Navy Journal*. "The game is destroyed or driven away; they are left to starve and there remains but one thing for them to do—fight while they can."

He also blamed ninety-nine out of a hundred Indian outbreaks on Indian agents and traders and broken faith by the government. He knew why Crazy Horse and Dull Knife did not want to come into "the white man's island," as they called the reservation, but he knew the government was set on it. What he did hope to do was make sure the reservation was located in the tribes' homelands.

General Crook sent word to Crazy Horse that if he would bring in his Sioux, they would get a reservation in their beloved Powder River country. Dull Knife and his band surrendered in April, and Crazy Horse and his people came to Fort Robinson in May.

After defeating Custer, Crazy Horse had been hunted for almost a year by vastly superior forces who had plenty of supplies and mounts, while the Sioux had shared the little they had with Dull Knife's destitute followers. Still, the Sioux rode into the fort with feathers and paint, singing proud songs. It was a last flourish Crook granted his valiant foes.

Most of them would regret surrender, for though General Crook tried to keep his promise of a Powder River reservation and even traveled to Washington to plead and argue, the white men took both the Powder River country and the Black Hills.

That September Crazy Horse was bayoneted to death by a soldier when he refused to enter a guardhouse, and in October General Crook had the unpleasant job of escorting the Sioux to their whittled-down remnants of land.

There were no free Indians left on all the Great Plains, north or south. Sitting Bull and a few Sioux had escaped into Canada, but in a few years they would rejoin their people and accept their fate.

Dull Knife and his Northern Cheyenne were sent south to live near their kinsmen, the Southern Cheyenne, just north of the Kiowa-Apache reservation. Dull Knife and his warriors protested.

They did not like that warmer region, and it was overcrowded. The buffalo were all gone. Why could they not stay here in their old home?

The government promised them plenty of food and supplies if they would go. Later Dull Knife claimed that he was promised that he and his band could come back north if, after a trial period, they did not like Oklahoma.

They did not like it. Though the Southern Cheyenne welcomed their northern brothers, there was pitifully little meat at the feast they gave the newcomers. The buffalo were gone, and all other game had been hunted close to extinction.

Instead of the ample supplies promised them, there was barely enough to live on. J. D. Miles, the agent in charge, told a Senate committee that the food he was given to feed his charges for a year would barely stretch through nine months, and at that, the beef was skin and bone with little good meat.

Homesick, always hungry, moved from their high cool lands to the sticky summer heat of Indian Territory, the Cheyenne immediately came down with fever and chills. Many died of measles. Mosquitoes buzzed everywhere, adding to the misery and disease. By the time the people had been on the reservation two months two-thirds of them were sick.

Winter brought an end to the heat but not to sickness. Forty-one Cheyenne died that season. There was only one doctor to care for five thousand Indians, and he had no medicine during the newcomers' time of greatest need, no quinine for the malaria or medicine for dysentery. Medicines and equipment he had needed and requested in the summer did not get to him till January.

The agent kept promising better times; beef, plows to make it easier to put in crops, schools that would teach the children to follow the white man's road. None of these was forthcoming. There was only hunger, sickness, filth, and the quarreling of people who were used to a free wandering life and now found themselves cramped close together in this sticky warm region they had never liked.

It seemed to Dull Knife that his people would all die. This life was not worth enduring. So it seemed also to Little Wolf, leader of another band and a very brave warrior.

Little Wolf, like Dull Knife was one of the Old Man Chiefs, the keeper of a sacred medicine bundle given to the tribe long ago by Sweet Medicine. He had traveled to Washington, where President Ulysses Grant gave him a peace medal but no help in making it possible for the Cheyenne to keep the peace, and he had served General Crook as a scout. Though he was fifty-seven now, he was still the fastest runner of the tribe and carried himself with the pride of a young man.

In July, Little Wolf, Dull Knife and other warriors went to the agent. Little Wolf said that this was not a good place for the Northern Cheyenne. They had seldom been sick in their land of pines and mountains, but everybody was sick here, and someone died nearly every day.

If the agent did not have the power to let them return, he could ask Washington for permission, or some of the Cheyenne would journey there and plead their desire.

"Stay another year," the agent coaxed. "Then if you still do not like it here, we will see what can be done."

"We cannot stay another year," said Little Wolf. "Before another year has passed, we may all be dead."

The talk settled nothing. The Cheyenne went back to their village and tried to decide what was best. Should they wait yet another year in this miserable place, hoping for food and help, or should they defy the agent, Washington and the Army and try to get back to their home mountains?

They were still trying to make their decision when troops came up with a howitzer and camped near them. Three young Cheyenne had run away, and the agent was afraid they would all go. He sent for Little Wolf and told him ten Cheyenne must be hostages until the three runaways were caught.

When Little Wolf heard this demand, he did not speak right away. He shook hands with the agent and with some Army officers who were present.

Then he said the three fugitives would never be caught and so the hostages would be held prisoner forever. It was not right that ten innocent men should lose their freedom. Hostages would not be given.

The agent told Little Wolf he would issue no rations unless hostages were given. The Cheyenne would starve till this was done.

"I cannot give you the ten men you wish, to be held for the three who have gone," Little Wolf said. "I will not give them." He reminded the agent that he had traveled to Washington and talked with President Grant, who had hoped the Indians and whites would be friends and stop fighting.

The agent insisted on the hostages yet again.

At last, when he saw nothing would help, Little Wolf shook hands again with the white men. He said he did not want blood spilled on the agency land, but that he was going north, back to his own country. If soldiers tried to stop them, they would fight.

Little Wolf went back to camp determined but full of sadness, for he knew the might of the Army. About 300 Cheyenne, including Dull Knife's band, listened with heavy hearts to his message. But they were Cheyenne, and they were proud. When they heard of the agent's demand for hostages, they all said that they would follow Dull Knife and Little Wolf to the north. At least they would die on their way back home.

It was so early next morning that the moon still shone when the Cheyenne stole out of their lodges and started a journey that has never been matched for courage or steadfast purpose.

There were babies carried by their mothers and old people who knew they would die on the journey, children who had to be warned to keep very quiet, and those who were so sick they could barely walk. There was Pretty Walker, the beautiful daughter of Little Wolf, and her brother who was called Wooden-thigh because he never got tired. Surely one of the strangest travelers was Yellow Swallow, the nine-year-old son of General Custer by a Cheyenne girl he had held captive after his massacre of Black Kettle's camp on the Washita, and had later abandoned.

Dull Knife led the people, though he was wracked with malaria and dysentery. Guarding the rear came Tangle Hair with his Dog Soldiers, whose duty it was to protect the people. More than 200 Cheyenne warriors had come south a year before; now there were fewer than 100 males over twelve years of age, and only 70 of these were on the march.

The Cheyenne left their lodges standing so that the soldiers would not see at once that they were gone. Once the people were some distance from the camp and soldiers, the remaining horses were led up and mounted by women with small children or those too weak to walk. The warriors had to be well mounted, of course, for they must fight off pursuers, who were sure to come.

When they stopped to rest, Little Wolf and Dull Knife told the warriors that they must not fire unless soldiers shot first, and they must not kill any settlers or other whites they met during their flight if this could possibly be avoided. This was not a war party. Its only aim was to get back to the Powder River country.

On the second evening, a guard signaled that many soldiers were coming. Little Wolf ordered the young men to get their weapons and horses but not to shoot until the whites did. He went to speak with the soldiers who had with them some Indian scouts and police from the agency.

Ghost Man, an Arapaho scout, rode forward to give a message from the agent. If the Cheyenne would return to the reservation, they would be given rations and treated well.

"I do not wish to fight with the whites," Little

Wolf said. "But we are going to our old home to stay there."

Ghost Man argued and pleaded, but Little Wolf did not waver. At last the scout gave up and rode back to the soldiers.

A bugle sounded. The troops opened fire. Tangle Hair and the Dog Soldiers charged, They fought till dark, and all through the night an occasional shot rang out.

Next morning the battle started early and lasted till afternoon when the troops started back down the river. They left dead two soldiers and Ghost Man, their messenger.

Several Cheyenne had been wounded, but none had been killed. They ate and rested. Next morning they started on.

Everyone was hungry. There was no meat except a few turtles and snakes, and they lived off choke-cherries, plums and half-ripe wild grapes.

This was not the prairie the Cheyenne had known, full of buffalo and game, vast and free-stretching far as the eye could see. Now there were telegraph poles rearing into the sky, ready to flash the location of the Cheyenne to soldiers, who could travel fast on monster trains hooting along the three East-West railroads scarring the region. The plains were now settled with whites who feared the Indians and would help the soldiers find them.

A few days after the first fight, more troopers attacked the Cheyenne on the Cimarron River. The Cheyenne drove them off after a short skirmish and camped for the night, too weary to move.

Next day the Indians marched on. About noon a

large command of soldiers and civilians—many of them buffalo hunters—attacked the Cheyenne, but after only a few shots, this force rode away, The puzzled Cheyenne traveled on. Late in the afternoon the big party came back with thirty or forty wagons. They went off one way to camp, and the Cheyenne moved down along a small creek and stopped there for the night.

Early next morning the troops advanced on the Indians, who fell back into some little hills for shelter. The soldiers drew the wagons up side by side into a long line. They dismounted near these and approached on foot, shooting as they came.

There were so many of them and their firing was so heavy that the younger warriors began to get excited, but Little Wolf called to them to hold their fire and keep steady.

"They have plenty of ammunition," he warned. "We have very little."

When the soldiers were close enough to make good targets, Little Wolf ordered the Cheyenne to shoot. One soldier fell. The others fell prone and shot from that position, which made them almost impossible to hit. The Cheyenne hoarded their precious cartridges and shot back just often enough to keep the troopers pinned down.

After a while a score of troopers eased back to the wagons. They mounted and tried to ride in from behind the Cheyenne, but Little Wolf led some warriors against them, killed one, and drove the rest back to the wagons. At this, the other troopers retreated to the wagons, got on their horses, and rode off while the wagons jolted after them pulled by mules the drivers whipped to a lope.

Dull Knife shouted to send the Cheyenne charging after the soldiers, but once the troopers were well on the run, Little Wolf called his warriors back. The Indian horses were not strong. They had a long journey ahead of them. Sweet as it was to defeat such a big force of troopers, it was more important to get away before even more whites caught up with them.

In their rush, the soldiers had left behind a box and a half of cartridges, which the ammunition-starved Cheyenne seized with delight.

It had been a long day of hard fighting, but Little Wolf knew that soldiers were probably closing in on them from all directions. The Cheyenne, exhausted and hungry but jubilant at their victory, moved camp that night.

Their good luck lasted. The next day they met a band of buffalo hunters. The Cheyenne did not hurt them, but they took their big heavy guns and ammunition and eighteen dead buffalo cows. At last they could eat!

Once the Cheyenne had crossed the Arkansas River, they camped on a small creek. Their tired horses needed to graze and rest, and unless meat was found and preserved against the coming winter, they would all starve and might as well be killed quickly by soldiers.

The buffalo were nothing like their former great numbers, but at least there were some. While the men hunted, the women put up breastworks on the knolls so that there would be some protection in case of attack. As the men brought in buffalo, women butchered in the clean Indian way that kept the meat on the hide till it could be cut up for drying.

For the first time on the journey, spirits were high and hopeful. Now they had strong buffalo meat to eat again. and enough was drying to get through the winter. The warriors had fought off several large forces of soldiers. Perhaps, after all, they might reach their own lands again and be allowed to stay there.

Laughter and singing warmed the camp while children played and the old dreamed of their homelands. Young warriors began to look again at favored maidens and steal a few words. Life could still be worth living if they could stay in the north, even on the reservation, even with buffalo dwindling.

While the Cheyenne hunted and rested, troops were being sent against them from all directions, and cavalry with four companies of infantry were being sent to guard the crossing on the Platte, which the Indians were expected to use. Orders from Washington were that unless the Cheyenne surrendered at once, giving up weapons and horses, they were to be attacked.

The Cheyenne had fought only when pushed to it, but Kansas settlers were terrified at what they believed was a great Indian uprising. Homesteaders, Texas trail drivers, and buffalo hunters joined with the troops to pursue the Cheyenne and surround their hunting camp.

The whites attacked, their bullets kicking up dust, but again Little Wolf calmed his warriors and did not let them fire until the enemy was close.

Then the Cheyenne shot so well that the whites fell back and took up firing from safer positions. This went on till night, when the soldiers went back to their wagons.

Little Wolf told his weary people that they must slip away in the darkness. Collecting the priceless dried meat, they traveled as fast and hard as they could for several days and did not really stop to rest till they were in southern Nebraska. They sighted troops, but these did not attack and the Indians moved on.

With scouts behind and on both sides, sometimes camping by day and traveling by night, sometimes going both day and night, the Cheyenne journeyed north. Their horses were worn out, so they took any that they found and killed some settlers' cattle for food. A few farmers tried to stop this and were killed by the young men.

The Cheyenne crossed the South Platte, the North Platte, and went into camp. It had been a terrible journey, but they were back in familiar lands now and felt safer. Dull Knife believed he and his band could winter at the Red Cloud Agency and perhaps be allowed to live there. While he went that way with his group, Little Wolf's band spent the winter in the sand hills, where they had good hunting of deer, antelope and cattle.

In the spring they started north toward the Powder, for Little Wolf distrusted all white men now and felt the farther he and his people got from them, the better. Sioux scouts reported Little Wolf's whereabouts to the Army, though, and the band was stopped by two troops of soldiers.

Fortunately, the officer in charge was a friend of Little Wolf's scouting days with General Crook and did not want to fight. He greeted Little Wolf with friendship, shaking his hand, and gave the Cheyenne rations.

For three days the soldiers and Indians camped together. The officer asked Little Wolf to give up the Cheyenne weapons and come into Fort Keogh.

Little Wolf trusted his friend. His Cheyenne gave up their arms and went to the fort. General Miles came out. He shook Little Wolf's hand and promised friendship, but he made the Cheyenne give up all their horses. Dismounted Indians were much easier to keep track of.

Not long after that, Miles asked Little Wolf if he and his warriors would like to enlist as scouts and help bring in those Sioux who were still at large. Little Wolf answered that he was tired of fighting. Perhaps he was thinking of the many Indian scouts, including some Cheyenne, who had fought and tracked his people as they traveled north.

Still, scouting was a life for warriors. They would have guns, horses, and excitement. Little Wolf talked it over with his men. Most decided to enlist, and Little Wolf joined with them. They saw some duty, but the Sioux came in before much time had passed, and the warriors had to settle into a quiet life on the reservation.

At least they were home.

Little Wolf lived twenty-five more years. He was buried on a hill, propped up by rocks and covered by them, his face turned toward his people as it had always been during his life.

After parting with Little Wolf's band, Dull Knife and his village moved toward the Red Cloud Agency where he hoped they would be permitted to stay. They met cavalry on the way, and Dull Knife told the commanding officer that his band would follow the soldiers to the agency. The officer took away the Indians' horses but gave rations, including sugar and coffee, which the Indians liked.

The Cheyenne woke next morning to find many more soldiers camped all around them, with the dreaded big guns. There was nothing they could do except give up their weapons as ordered. Men were allowed to keep their bows and knives, and some women managed to take guns apart and hide them in their clothes, for they were not searched as the warriors were.

For ten days the soldiers camped in a guarding circle around the Indians while Dull Knife tried to persuade the officer to take them to the agency, which had been moved some distance down the stream. The officer, though, had strict orders to bring the Cheyenne into Fort Robinson.

The argument ran on, while tempers rose. Almost every night more soldiers came. They began building breastworks. The Cheyenne dug rifle pits, but this was fairly useless since they had managed to hide only five guns.

Other officers had come to pressure Dull Knife and his warriors. One of these whites promised that if the Indians would come into Fort Robinson and surrender, they would be given plenty of rations and sent to the agency as they desired.

Dull Knife finally agreed to surrender at the fort. After all, there was not much else to do unless many Indians were to be slaughtered by the soldiers' cannon and guns.

Army wagons hauled the women and children. At first the horseless men walked, but the snow was deep and they were ordered into the wagons.

Soldiers marched in two files on either side of the caravan. More were ahead of it, and still more behind. About sundown the Indians reached Fort Robinson. They were taken into a long building where they were counted and the names of the leading men were written down. They were fed and allowed to rest that night.

Next morning some officers and Sioux scouts came in to talk with them. Tangle Hair spoke both Cheyenne and Sioux, so he spoke Sioux to the interpreter, who told the whites what was said. Then the officers' words passed through the interpreter and Tangle Hair to the Cheyenne.

The post commander told the Cheyenne that they must stay at Fort Robinson for three months while the government decided what to do with them. If they were peaceful, they could go freely around the fort and even go into the hills, but by suppertime each night they must all be back at the barracks where they were to live.

"If one man of you deserts or runs away, you will not be treated like this anymore," warned the commander. "You will all be held responsible for him."

Dull Knife rose to speak for his people. "We are back on our own ground and have stopped fighting. We have found the place we started to come to."

For some weeks all went well. The Cheyenne were given plenty of food. They could gather red willow bark at the stream to smoke in pipes and sage for purification rites. The doctor gave them quinine for the malaria some still suffered and did what he could for the exhausted, nearly starved children and their parents.

For the first time in almost three years, they had

plenty to eat—mush, molasses, thick stew with lots of good meat. The women could wash clothing in the stream without being afraid of being caught by soldiers; there was time to dress skins and make moccasins and line the children's cradleboards with soft rabbit fur.

The young people played games with balls or hoops and sticks. Sometimes the young men were allowed to race the soldiers while on-lookers cheered and made wagers.

When the weather was bad, the Cheyenne played games inside. The soldiers taught the men how to play cards. At night there was singing, and often soldiers came to the dances at the barracks and gave presents to the Cheyenne girls—beads, ribbons, rings and other trinkets pretty girls like.

In spite of the temporary relief and pleasantness, the Cheyenne were prisoners and felt it keenly. The older ones had been through too many grievous experiences with the whites to believe that this easy life would continue.

As time passed and the weeks went by, they knew that soon the government would have decided what to do with them. The Cheyenne felt sick at the idea of returning to the south. Many said they would not go. And they all remembered that it was here that Crazy Horse had been treacherously bayoneted little more than a year ago.

After two months one Cheyenne slipped away to join his wife who was living at the Pine Ridge Agency. When he did not return, the Cheyenne were locked in the barracks and sentries were posted all around. The runaway warrior was brought back, but now a terrible time began for these people who had already been through so much.

The government had decided that the Cheyenne must go south, back to Indian Territory. The officers now began trying to persuade them to submit. Red Cloud, the Sioux chief, tried to convince them that nothing but death could come of resistance.

But Dull Knife and his people would not consent. They said the south was not healthful for them and they would never go back.

"You may kill me here," said Dull Knife, speaking for his people. "But you cannot make me go back."

General Crook wired the Indian Department that it was very cold and it would be inhuman to move the Indians in such weather. They did not have enough clothing, and temperatures were often at zero and even forty degrees below.

Added to the Cheyenne's woes was a new commander at the post, a Captain Henry W. Wessels, who was disliked by everybody and was called the Flying Dutchman by the soldiers for the way he dashed around meddling in everything. He made the Cheyenne women clean up the grounds of the post and was always coming in and out of the barracks.

When the Cheyenne refused to go south, he ordered them locked in the barracks, and on the third of January he told them they must make the move. They said they would not.

The government ordered Wessels to begin their journey south, even after he reported that the Cheyenne would rather die. When no threats or pleading could change their decision, Wessels told them there would be no more food or wood for fires till they bowed to the government's will. He was sure that in a few days the strongest warriors would be defeated by the suffering of small children and the sick and aged.

The Cheyenne were already in tatters, for no warm winter clothing had been sent for them. They wrapped themselves as best they could in their shabby blankets and kept small fires going with the crude furniture and the floorboards. They had a few scraps of tallow and grain, and these were given to the children, who did not cry while awake but wept softly from cold and hunger in their broken sleep.

For five days there was no food. Wessels asked if they would go now; when Dull Knife said they would not, even the drinking water was stopped.

Wessels did ask the women and children to come out. He promised that they would be fed and put in a warm place. But the Cheyenne drove the messenger away. Whatever happened would happen to them all.

They scraped frost from the windows to wet their tongues. Thirst was added to the miseries of starvation and freezing. Wessels persuaded three of the leaders to come out and parley; but when they said the Cheyenne would not obey the government's orders, they were put in irons and taken to the guardhouse.

Now the Cheyenne had been without food for eight days, without water for three. Some were delirious and staggered when they tried to walk. Some tried to jump out of the barracks so that they would be shot and have an easy death, but friends held them back.

Wessels could not believe that any people would endure such torture without bending. He called on Dull Knife to come out.

Dull Knife answered that his people would never go south. "The only way to get us there is to come in here with clubs and knock us on the head and drag us out and take us down there dead."

The interpreter had a special friend among the Cheyenne and begged him to come out and be saved, but the young warrior said that he would die with his band.

Now the desperate Cheyenne talked together and decided to break out that night. They put together the weapons they had managed to hide, five rifles and eleven six-shooters. Few of their possessions were left, but the most precious tribal relics—things which would remind any survivors of what it had meant to be Cheyenne—were to be taken.

There was the ancient stone buffalo horn that was sacred to the society of Dog Soldiers, some fine quillwork, and the lance heads of the tribal bands. Great Eyes, an old warrior, called his thirteen-year-old nephew and gave him his shield trimmed with eagle feathers and grizzly bear claws, reminding him how proud was its past, how many arrows and bullets it had turned.

The best shots took the firearms. Some Cheyenne had knives, and those who had nothing else tore up floorboards to use as clubs. There were 149 Cheyenne in the barracks. Only 46 of these were males between eleven and eighty years of age.

Outside, a very heavy guard had been placed. As the winter day faded, the Cheyenne painted their faces and put on their best clothing and fancy moccasins. They went around and kissed each other for a last time.

"It is true that we must die," they told each other. "But we will not die shut up here like dogs; we will die on the prairie; we will die fighting."

Most did expect to die out there in the snow, but fast-running men were entrusted to speed away with some of the children, and a few strong women with them, in the hope that at least these could carry on the tribe, find refuge somewhere, perhaps with Red Cloud or Little Wolf.

The moon was bright and full as it had been four months ago when they crept out of their lodges in Indian Territory and fled north. So many had died since then! And now it seemed they all might, simply because they wanted to live in their own beloved high country.

They stacked saddles and other gear under the windows so that they could quickly climb out when the time came. An armed warrior stood at each window. If anyone was to escape, the outbreak must be sudden and well planned.

Little Shield, a leader of the Dog Soldiers, gave the signal about ten o'clock by firing at a guard and knocking out a window. The other warriors did the same. Cheyenne jumped from all the windows, making for the bluffs two miles from the post. On the way they crossed the spring where they threw themselves down to drink in spite of the bullets, for the garrison had roused at the firing and was now after the fugitives.

Tangle Hair and four Dog Soldiers formed a rear guard and sprang around, taunting and shooting at the soldiers, trying to hold them back to give the other Cheyenne a chance to reach cover. All these warriors were killed except for Tangle Hair.

He was lucky. Some soldiers who knew and liked him found him wounded, took him to their quarters, and got the doctor. But most wounded Cheyenne, even women and children, were shot as the soldiers caught up with them.

Some soldiers did try to take prisoners because they sympathized with these brave people who only wanted to live in their homelands. Many of the soldiers had danced with the pretty Indian girls, joked and played cards with the young men, and given candy to the children they were now ordered to pursue.

The Cheyenne ran up the valley along the creek, often breaking through the ice and getting wet. When a warrior fell, a woman or boy caught up his weapon and fought. It was almost as light as day with snow reflecting moonlight, so the Cheyenne could not hide—not till they reached the trees and bluffs.

Women burdened with children fell behind. Dull Knife's beautiful daughter, called Princess by the soldiers who had admired her, was carrying someone else's baby and was shot along with five other women and several children. All the way from the barracks to the bluffs stretched a trail marked by Cheyenne dead, mostly women, babies and small children who could not run fast.

Still, some Cheyenne reached the sandstone bluffs and could shoot from cover. The whites fell back, not liking their turn at being easy targets. They took sixty-five captives back to the post, many of them wounded.

Of those Cheyenne left in the bluffs, some hid overnight. Next day they would fight and die or be taken prisoner. But others perilously made their way up the bluff in the night and pushed westward in the freezing cold, weak, starving, some wounded, some carrying children.

When day dawned, soldiers came out with wagons to bring in the dead. They found about 50 frozen bodies and took them back to the post. Captain Wessels went to his 65 prisoners and said, "Now will you go south?"

A wounded girl dragged herself to her feet. "No, we will not go back," she scornfully told the white officer. "We will die rather. You have killed most of us, why do you not go ahead now and finish the work?"

Four troops of cavalry hunted the 34 Cheyenne who had scaled the bluff during the night. There were 20 men and 14 women and children. Many were wounded, some were badly lamed by frostbite. Still they escaped into the Badlands. They hoped to reach Pine Ridge where friends would hide and feed them.

When the soldiers overtook them, the Cheyenne would take cover and fight, then slip away in the night. Their first food in days was the meat of a dead cavalry horse.

For an unbelievable twelve days they eluded the soldiers, but at last they were trapped on the plain, surrounded on all sides by the four troops. The Cheyenne took refuge in an old buffalo wallow.

Wessels called on then, to give up. In answer, the Cheyenne fired and began to sing the death chants made when they expected to die.

Two troops of cavalry kept steady fire centered on the Cheyenne while the other two groups charged close by them, firing from opposite sides.

When the troopers fell back to reload, three warriors jumped from the pit and rushed their attackers with knives and one empty pistol. They were killed at once. The troopers swept by again, firing, and when they had finished, all the men were dead and seven women and children. Five women and children were wounded but would live, and only two had somehow escaped that withering fire unhurt.

Dull Knife, with his wife, son, daughter-in-law, grandchild and Red Bird, the young boy who was carrying his uncle's wonderful shield, had been separated from the main group of fugitives and had hidden in a hole in some rocks. Dull Knife did not know that one of his daughters and one of his sons were dead. He kept his small group hidden ten days. Then they made their way to the Pine Ridge Agency after eighteen days, traveling by dark and eating roots, some sinew their women had hidden, and their moccasins.

At Pine Ridge, William Rowland, who had sometimes interpreted for them, took them in and cared for them.

Some newspapermen had been along during the hounding of the desperate Cheyenne. When their stories appeared, the nation was shocked and angry, bitterly ashamed. Protests flooded Washington. General Crook ordered an investigation of the whole affair.

Under public pressure, the Bureau of Indian Affairs finally allowed fifty-eight Cheyenne to go live with the Sioux at the Pine Ridge Agency. The wounded, frostbitten women, children and badly crippled men were loaded into wagons and taken to the home which had cost them so much.

There were only seven reasonably able-bodied men left, and they were sent back to Kansas, along

with their families, to stand trial for the few white settlers that had been killed on the Cheyenne's way north.

Defense funds poured in from all over the country and lawyers defended Tangle Hair and his compan-
ions without charge. The court dismissed the case for
lack of evidence, but for a while these Cheyenne had
to stay at the hated reservation in Indian Territory.

Soon, though, they were allowed to go north and
rejoin their broken people. They took with them the
sacred buffalo hat, and when the remnant of their
band came to meet them, they sang in joy of reunion.

The Tongue River Reservation was set aside for
the Northern Cheyenne, and here the bands of Dull
Knife and Little Wolf were together again. The buffalo
were gone and they were sometimes hungry, but at
least they were home.

Dull Knife died about 1883 and was buried on a
high butte above the Rosebud River.

Until recent action by Indians themselves,
Indian children have not been taught the proud history of their tribes, yet in the history of mankind
there were no braver people than Dull Knife's
Cheyenne.

Surely their descendants have a right to live with
strength and dignity in their own land.

FURTHER SUGGESTED READING

Chalfont, William Y., *Cheyennes and Horse Soldiers*.
     Norman, University of Oklahoma Press, 1989.
Deloria Jr., Vine, *Custer Died For Your Sins*. New York,
     Avon, 1970.

Grinnell, George Bird, *By Cheyenne Campfires*. New
  Haven, Yale University Press, 1962.

—— *The Cheyenne Indians*, Volumes 1 and 2. Lincoln,
  University of Nebraska Press, 1972.

—— *The Fighting Cheyennes*. Norman, University of
  Oklahoma Press, 1958.

Powell, Peter J., *Sweet Medicine*. Norman, University of
  Oklahoma Press, 1979.

Sandoz, Mari, *Cheyenne Autumn*. New York, Avon, 1953.

THE APACHE

Long Prisoners of War

By the time American trappers ventured into the mountains in present-day New Mexico and Arizona the Apache were dreaded by all settled people, whether Mexican or Pueblo Indian. Though described as "gentle" by early Spanish explorers, it did not take the Apache long to tire of being branded and worked as slaves in Spanish fields and mines.

They retaliated by raiding missions, towns, mining villages and ranches, striking deep into Mexico for plunder, horses, mules, cattle, women and children for slaves, and anything striking their fancy that could be carried away.

There were six different tribes of Apache, not counting their close kin, the Navajo. Lipan and Kiowa-Apache lived on the plains of Texas, Oklahoma and Kansas, where Coronado found them following the buffalo. They were more like the Comanche and Kiowa than their Apache cousins of the mountains and mesas to the west. Also resembling Plains Indians were the Mescalero, who roamed from south-central New Mexico into the mountains of Texas' Big Bend and northern Mexico. The Jicarilla were at home in northeastern New Mexico and southeastern Colorado; the Western Apache lived in eastern Arizona; and the Chiricahua ranged southeastern Arizona, southwestern New Mexico and northern Mexico.

The Yuma or Mojave Apache were not Apache at all, but Yavapai, who indulged in numerous depredations for which Apache were blamed. Even the name Apache was not what they called themselves but was probably the Zuñi word for "enemy."

The Western Apache divided into five main groups, which separated into twenty bands usually named after the region where they lived, such as the Bald Mountain Band or the Creek Canyon Band. The Chiricahua di-

Map 3   Present-Day Reservations

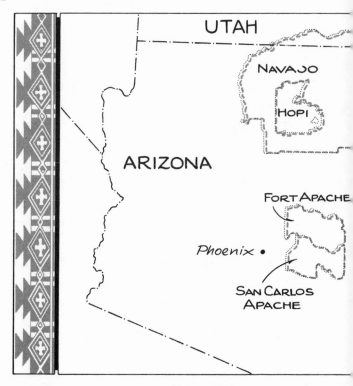

vided into Eastern, Southern and Western Bands.

None of these groups was numerous. It is estimated that when the Americans entered Apache country, there were around 4,000 Western Apache and about 1,000 Chiricahua.

There was no political or military connection between the bands. Except for their plains relatives, the Apache lived in rugged country gashed by canyons and ridged by mountain ranges where many people could not live together without running short of food. The bands split into local groups rather like big families. Each of these small units had their own headman and carried on their wars, raids and ordinary life without knowing what the closest group down the creek or up the canyon was doing.

This lack of a central political military power baffled Spaniards, Mexicans and Americans in turn.

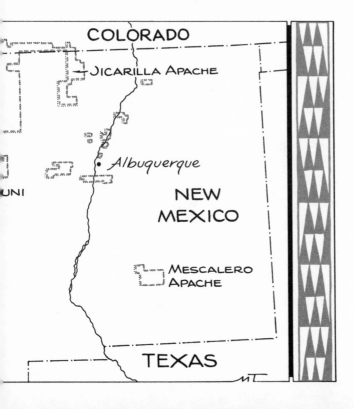

A treaty or agreement with one chief did not bind the other forty or so headman. This made it impossible to deal with Apache as a whole—not that they were eager to deal with more strangers!

They had been invited to "pinole treaties" where their dried corn was treated with strychnine; they had been branded and worked as slaves by the Spaniards; and the Mexican government paid bounty on scalps of men, women and children.

In 1835 some trappers on the upper Gila led by an Englishman named James Johnson invited the Apache to a big party, promising to give out whiskey, blankets and flour. About thirty-five Indians came. While they were looking over their presents, Johnson set off a howitzer loaded with nails, broken chains, bullets and other shrapnel-like junk.

About twenty Apache were killed at once. Trappers finished off the wounded, except for a few who managed to get away. When they told their story, chiefs like Mangas Coloradas, who had usually been friendly to the whites, no longer checked their warriors. Dozens of innocent whites were killed, though Johnson escaped to California without collecting from the Sonoran government $100 for each man, $50 for each woman, and $25 for each dead Apache child.

Other bounty hunters would earn their living from turning in Apache scalps, though. In some cases they turned in Mexican hair. White men and Mexicans who called the Apache "cruel, treacherous and thieving" earned the description themselves.

The United States took over much Apache territory after the Mexican War, and five years later the 1853 Gadsden Purchase placed the rest of Apache country under United States control, or lack of it.

By treaty with Mexico, the United States undertook to stop Apache raids into Mexico, a centuries' old custom that was not going to be easily broken. As American miners, trappers, ranchers and settlers pushed into the region, mostly treating the Apache like dangerous wild animals, the Apache struck back with raids and killings.

Even so, there were white individuals who got on well with the Apache. One was Tom Jeffords who was superintendent of mail between Fort Bowie and Tucson. When his drivers were being picked off by Apache, Jeffords went by himself to find Cochise, great war leader of the Chiricahua. He asked Cochise to let his drivers carry out their work. The two men became friends and later were blood brothers. The mail wagons were never again molested, even after the Camp Grant massacre in 1871, when a Tucson mob of whites and Mexicans slaughtered 128 peaceful Apache men, women and children who had come in to settle on a reservation.

Two months after this frightful event, while the Apache spread death and terror throughout the Gila country, General George Crook arrived in Arizona. Called the "terrible and just," Crook was in many ways like the Indians he had to subdue. To the end of his life, he was to use his influence on their behalf.

He lived simply, neither drank nor smoked, never wore a uniform when he could avoid it, and braided his beard in pigtails to keep it neat on campaign. His favorite recreation was to go off by himself to hunt. That first season in Arizona, though, gave him no leisure.

Through the scorching summer heat, he scouted

the Gila watershed, marching his men through Apache country, talking to Apache and offering peace.

He told them the whites had come to stay, but that if the Apache would settle to farm and raise horses and cattle, there would be plenty of land and food for all races. He promised that bad whites would be punished if they wronged Apache, just as Apache would suffer for raids or murders.

He was making good progress when a peace commission was sent from Washington and Crook was ordered to stand back. The two commissioners knew nothing about Apache or the background of the troubles. After a few talks with a few Apache, including one most ambiguous conversation with the aging Cochise, the commissioners wrote back to Washington that they had made peace and went on to other matters.

Crook, who had been powerless to enforce his earlier warnings while the commissioners were around, found the Apache had decided he had no authority to back up his words. During the year after the so-called peace, Apache killed a hundred people in more than sixty attacks. Washington demanded of Crook why he couldn't control the Indians after all the fine work of the peace commission.

Dividing his command into five separate units, Crook sent word that those Apache who surrendered would be fed and well treated, but those who remained defiant would be pursued till they gave up or were killed. Any Apache who wished to join up as a scout was to be enrolled, and great effort was to be made to spare all women and children.

Gradually, Crook wore the Apache down. They

learned that he could be their best friend or most formidable enemy. Soon most of the Western Apache came in to live on the San Carlos Reservation on the Gila and at Fort Apache in the White Mountains.

If Crook had been allowed to handle the Apache, there might well have been no later uprisings. They called him Gray Fox and believed what he said. He got them started in stock raising and showed them better ways to farm.

All mountain and desert-dwelling Apache got considerable food from hunting and from wild fruits, seeds, nuts and roots. One important food was the "head" or the yucca or mescal, which was cut from the center of the spiky leaves and then baked several days in a pit lined with steaming rocks. This could be eaten fresh, tasting like stringy molasses, or could be dried and stored. In addition to these foods, the Western Apache had learned to grow corn, beans and squash. Now Crook hoped to teach them how to grow enough to feed not only themselves but also the Army.

Naturally, if the Indians fed themselves and sold extra crops to the Army, it meant a loss of money to contractors and the all-too-many Indian Bureau officials who profited from selling to the reservation and Army at high prices. In spite of howls and pressure from these men, Crook went on with his plan to make the Apache self-supporting and show them that farming paid better than raids.

With broken tools and fire-sharpened sticks, the Indians dug a five-mile-long irrigation ditch at Camp Verde and soon had sixty acres in crops. The cavalry officers joined in the project and built a waterwheel from old packing boxes. At Camp Apache the Indians grew 250 tons of corn and 15 tons of beans, using only broken hoes and sticks.

Most Apache were not so fond of raiding that they couldn't see the advantage of having plenty of food and getting paid for any surplus they produced. Besides, if an Apache didn't want to farm, he could enlist as a scout for Crook.

Meanwhile, the Chiricahua who followed Cochise had been given a reservation in the Dragoon and Huachuca Mountains in their home range in southeastern Arizona. They were not under Crook's jurisdiction because of the treaty General Oliver Otis Howard of the peace commission had made with Cochise. Cochise was ailing and could not control his young men, who kept raiding into Mexico. The eastern Chiricahua lived in their western New Mexico lands, while the southern Chiricahua had thrown in their lot with Cochise.

At this time and, unfortunately, for a long time after, the Indian Bureau was full of men who profiteered off the Indians. Some Indian agents starved the people they were supposed to look after and sold the supplies to whites. Contractors sold inferior food, clothing and blankets at sky-high prices. All too often Indian Bureau officials owned contracting or trading businesses and gave these concerns contracts to feed the Army or reservations.

These cheats were furious at Crook's success in showing the Apache how to feed themselves and the military. They put pressure on Washington for the Apache to be moved to the mouth of the San Carlos River where, the profiteers hoped, they couldn't feed themselves.

Crook protested. He said dust and malaria would sicken the mountain-dwelling Apache. But the move was ordered and the Apache had to settle on the San Carlos. White farmers were taking up all the water rights, and miners seemed to get the rest.

Then, just to make it a thorough mess, Washington decided *all* Apache must go live on the San Carlos reservation. None of the Chiricahua liked this, nor did the Western Apache. Each band wanted to stay in the region known and loved by its members. But Crook had to bring in the Chiricahua in 1874.

This firm, just man might have managed to make even this situation bearable for the Apache had he been allowed to stay, but in 1875 the War Department ordered him north to settle the Cheyenne and Sioux. It was a bad day for the Apache—and Arizona and northern Mexico—when he left.

For the next nine or ten years, the Chiricahua would be off and on the reservation. Once they broke out, they were impossible to catch, even burdened as they were with women, children and the aged.

An example of their incredible toughness is old Nana. In his seventies, half-blind, and severely crippled with rheumatism, this old chief led forty Chiricahua and Mescalero on a two-month raid in the summer of 1881. While covering more than 1,000 miles of desert from Mexico through southwestern New Mexico, his band fought and won eight battles, killed and wounded many enemy, and captured scores of horses and mules.

That was the summer when a medicine man promised that their most powerful dead leaders were coming back to lead the Chiricahua Apache against the whites and restore to them all their old land. Soldiers tried to arrest this prophet. The Apache rebelled, and men were killed on both sides, including the medicine man. The Chiricahua, led by Juh and Geronimo, killed the agency chief of police, cut off the agent's head, used it for a football, and left the reservation, heading for Mexico.

There they lost half their fighting men in a battle with Mexican troops. The survivors refuged high in the Sierra Madre. That same summer about fifty Western Apache fled the hated San Carlos reservation, killing and plundering till the soldiers caught up with them and killed those who did not surrender.

With all of Arizona and New Mexico in terror, Crook was sent back to Arizona to restore order. He wasted no time at headquarters and was in the saddle the next day, headed for Camp Apache. The Apache came to his council, for though some of his old friends were dead, many remembered him as the Gray Fox who kept his word. He asked them for their side of the story.

They asked why all the good officers had been sent away and why he had left them. One Apache said of the present officers: "We couldn't make out what they wanted; one day they seemed to want one thing, the next day something else. Perhaps we were to blame, perhaps they were; but, anyhow, we hadn't any confidence in them."

All the Apache lamented their friends among Crook's old command, and told how their fields had been destroyed and they had been forced down to San Carlos where, as one of Crook's lieutenants said, "the water is salt and the air poison, and one breathes a mixture of sand blizzards and more flies than were ever supposed to be under the care of the great flygod Beelzebub."

There they could be fed miserable rations while the Indian agent filled his pockets with the government money that was supposed to buy them adequate food. He also made them work in the coal mines and generally was so corrupt that even the Federal Grand Jury of Arizona condemned him and blamed him for Apache outbreaks and restlessness. As a result of this investigation, the agent, the Inspector General of the Indian Bureau, and the Commissioner of Indian Affairs all lost their positions.

General Crook rode through all the territory, hearing the problems of the Western Apache and promising them that if they would stay on the reservation, they could settle wherever they wished within its boundaries and the Army would protect them from encroaching miners and farmers, as well as from rebellious Indians. They could raise their own food and sell what was left over. They could have their own judges and police force. Any man who didn't want to farm could become a scout.

With Crook back, the Western Apache quickly settled down. At the end of Crook's first year among them, Indians near Camp Apache had raised 2,500,000 pounds of corn, 180,000 pounds of beans, as well as wheat, barley, potatoes, melons, pumpkins and squash. They sold much of the barley to feed government horses and mules and cut and sold 400 tons of hay and 300 cords of wood to the Quartermaster Department.

For at least a little while, there was peace in Arizona. But the Chiricahua were still hiding in Mexico. There were about 600 of them, but no more than 150 were warriors or boys who were big enough to fight. As warm weather came in the spring of 1883 a chief named Chato led 26 Chiricahua on raids in Mexico and across the border. He soon had 4,000 Mexican troops and 500 U.S. soldiers after him.

Stealing fresh horses when their tired ones gave out, Chato's band fought across New Mexico and Arizona and back into Mexico, covering close to a hundred miles a day and losing only two men. Meanwhile, Geronimo was leading raids through Sonora.

Crook knew that the only way to put an end to this was to follow the Chiricahua to their refuge in the Sierra Madre. He went by train to Sonora and Chihuahua and talked to Mexican civil and military leaders. They weren't happy at having U.S. troops inside their borders but decided it was better than being unwilling hosts to the Apache. The Mexican leaders agreed to help Crook and raised no objection to his crossing the border.

Crook got back to Arizona and collected 200 Indian scouts, 40 troopers and 10 officers. Leaving some cavalrymen at the border, he crossed into Mexico.

All along the valley that led to the mountains from where the Apache struck, Crook's men found the villagers terrified. Pushing up into the jagged ridges which were so steep that five pack mules fell to their deaths, Crook found the Apache's abandoned stronghold and signs of retreat.

Crook's mounted troopers could not follow the deft-footed Apache farther. His scouts told him that the cavalry and pack train should stop while the scouts and a few white officers pursued the Chiricahua. If the Chiricahua were found in such a strong position that more men were needed, the cavalry could be sent for.

Several days later the scouts caught up with two camps, which fought and scattered. A captive girl said the Chiricahua were badly shaken when they saw that most of the force pursuing them was Apache. Eluding them was different from giving white troopers the slip. The girl felt that most of the Chiricahua would surrender now that they had been chased around their Mexican refuge by Apache, who knew the same ways of fighting, tracking and living off the country.

Crook gave her food and sent her along with a captive boy to tell her people they would be treated fairly if they gave up. Within a few days Chiricahua began giving themselves up, including one leader, Chihuahua.

Apache warriors kept coming in. It was more like a village than an Army camp, with children playing, women busy, and the men playing their flutes or single-stringed fiddles of yucca root. The soldiers killed a few ponies to feed the people, who also roasted mescal.

Horse and mule meat was preferred to beef by the Apache, who, except for their prairie cousins, never became horse Indians. They would ride a horse to death and then eat him, steal another mount, and repeat the process.

Geronimo and Chato were still on the loose, raiding Mexico. When they heard that most Chiricahua had been taken and that Mexican forces were going to help Crook track down all the Apache still out, they surrendered. They were allowed to collect their followers, which took some time, but eventually they came in.

In June, Crook brought about four hundred Chiricahua back to Arizona. He divided them into small groups, which he settled with the farming Western Apache on the San Carlos reservation. Amazingly, Geronimo turned out to be one of the best farmers.

Though his name grew to be synonymous with the Apache, Geronimo was not rated very high among his people. It was said that he would rather talk than eat, and he loved food. Still, he would lead his small band on the last desperate Apache raids.

Now that all the Arizona Apache were settled, Crook tried to help them become self-supporting, but the Indian agent, over whom Crook had no authority, had other ideas. The agent wouldn't even permit the digging of an irrigation ditch, a necessity for more and better crops.

Even though most Chiricahua were eventually taken to live in the higher wooded area of Fort Apache, they were still a long way from home. Unlike the Western Apache, they had never done any farming, and they tired of it quickly for the most part. Also they resented Crook's order that they must not make or drink tiswin, a potent mescal drink. Nor did they think white men had a right to tell them they could not cut off the nose of an unfaithful wife, which was the practice.

Added to all these irritations was rivalry between

Chato and Geronimo, which split the tribe apart. In May, 1885, Geronimo's faction went on a big tiswin spree. About a quarter of the Chiricahua followed him off the reservation including important leaders like Naiche, Cochise's son, Mangus, son of Mangas Coloradas, and Chihuahua. Of the 144 Chiricahua only 43 were men or boys old enough to fight.

Chihuahua and Mangus seem to have been frightened into flight by Geronimo's telling them that an Army officer had been killed and that they would all hang for it. When they learned that Lieutenant Britton Davis was not dead, Mangus and Chihuahua with their followers broke away from Geronimo's party.

But Geronimo pushed for Mexico, killing all the way. During the next months, while troopers chased him back and forth across the border, Geronimo's band killed 73 white civilians, 10 soldiers, 12 peaceful Indians, and perhaps 100 Mexican citizens.

Crook put guards at water holes and mountain passes along the border and kept constant patrols out, but it would have taken thousands of men to guard all the Mexican border through New Mexico and Arizona.

Late in 1885 Crook sent a select group of Chiricahua and Western Apache scouts across the border with a few white officers. They tracked the hostiles and hit them hard in January. Geronimo asked for peace and promised to meet Crook in two months, at the Canyon de los Embudos, where Sonora and Chihuahua meet beneath the joint borders of Arizona and New Mexico.

A scream of outrage went up from the newspapers. How could Crook take the word of an Apache renegade? However, late in March, when Crook rode into the canyon, Geronimo and his band were there.

Geronimo made a lot of excuses for why he had broken off from the reservation, but Crook was stern with him. Geronimo and his main warriors had killed many innocent people. To be sure they kept the peace this time, they would be sent east for two years, along with their families. If Geronimo did not agree to this, he and his band would be hunted down and killed, even if it took fifty years.

After a night to think it over, Geronimo surrendered. Unfortunately, just across the border was a white bootlegger named Tribollet. He sold the Apache mescal and a lot of terrifying stories, telling them about the punishment they were going to get at San Carlos. Tribollet, like all too many traders and bootleggers, wanted to keep the Indians hostile, since this brought in troops who had to buy things.

Geronimo and most of his band rode off as fast as they could. Crook sent soldiers after them, and about 80 Chiricahua gave up and went along to the reservation. But Geronimo, Naiche and 30 others kept going into Mexico.

Crook still believed that once Geronimo sobered up, he would accept Crook's word over that of a bootlegger and give himself up. Crook's military superiors criticized his handling of the whole situation and added that prisoners being sent east must not be promised a return to Arizona.

After some dispute, Crook said that he had used his best judgment and experience and that if he could not act upon them, he wanted to be transferred.

He was sent to Nebraska. General Nelson Miles was assigned the job of bringing Geronimo in. For five months 5,000 troops and 500 Apache scouts chased Geronimo's tiny group of 33 around the country, much like a herd of elephants trying to catch a mouse. Mexican troops combed the other side of the border, but the Apache eluded everyone.

Miles did have some Chiricahua close at hand, though, who didn't have to be captured. These were the three hundred who had stayed on the reservation all this time. Many had served as scouts in expeditions against Geronimo, but Miles didn't trust them, or perhaps he just liked to look as if he were doing something important.

He assembled them to receive rations and loaded them on trains bound for prison in Florida. The eighty Chiricahua who had surrendered to Crook in March had already been shipped east. So now all the Chiricahua, who had kept their word and trusted the whites, were exiled prisoners perishing of fevers and illness, while only Geronimo, who had repeatedly broken his word and caused trouble, stayed at large.

Geronimo and his band were tired, though, and winter was coming. He sent word that he wished to talk surrender. Two Chiricahua scouts and one of Crook's experienced men, Lieutenant Charles B. Gatewood, went to parley with Geronimo. On September 3, 1886, Gatewood brought the Apache in, except for a half a dozen who hid out in the Sierra Madre.

Geronimo's band soon left for Florida on a heavily guarded prison train. With him, unbelievably, went the two scouts who had risked their lives to arrange his final surrender!

Five hundred Chiricahua had been sent as prisoners of war to Florida. Less than a quarter of these had done anything to deserve it, but the whole tribe was punished for the raids of Geronimo. They were never to go back to their old home.

Lieutenant John G. Bourke, who had served with Crook through the Apache campaigns, wrote angrily: "There is no more disgraceful page in the history of our relations with the American Indians than that which conceals the treachery visited upon the Chiricahuas who remained faithful in their allegiance to our people."

Though the warriors had been told they could live with their families in Florida, the women and children stayed at Fort Marion while most of the men were kept at the old fort at St. Augustine. Geronimo and sixteen of his followers lived under guard at Fort Pickens, several hundred miles away from the other Apache.

Imprisonment and dampness had a terrible effect on these people who were used to roving free among their dry deserts and mountains. They longed to be where they could "see the sun without climbing a pine tree."

Within a year, 55 had died. General Crook spoke and wrote in their behalf. So did many other people, though any suggestion that they be sent back to their homeland stirred loud protest from the citizens of Arizona and New Mexico. In 1887 they were shifted to Alabama, except for the Fort Pickens prisoners, who were at last reunited with their families, mostly through the work of the Indian Rights Association. In May, 1888, the Fort Pickens group was allowed to join the rest of the Chiricahua. Life was better for them in Alabama than in Florida, but they were homesick and easy prey to illness. By 1890, 120 of the small tribe had died in captivity.

Crook visited them early in 1890. Chato, Chihuahua and many others flocked close to greet the Gray Fox, shake hands, and laugh in delight. Crook inspected the school, talked for some time with the people, and promised to do what he could for them. The honorable old soldier was furious that his loyal scouts had met the same punishment as Geronimo.

He wrote up his report, and a few weeks later the battle began in Congress between those who favored leaving the Apache where they were and those who felt they should be given land in the Indian Territory, which would be more like their native region.

General Miles, supported by most of the Western press, declared that Indian Territory was too close to the Chiricahua's home range and that his treatment of the tribe had been prudent and justified. Crook had plenty of evidence to dispute this. The whole history of the Chiricahua wars was dragged out. Old reports and correspondence were studied by Congress.

While this dragged on, Crook was feeling sick. He died in March, 1890. There is small doubt that his worry and efforts for the Chiricahua led to his fatal heart failure at sixty-two years of age.

Throughout the West, Indians whom he had fought and then tried to help mourned Crook, but most of all, he was wept for by the Apache, who let down their hair and wailed like children.

The Chiricahua spent four more years in Alabama. At last, in 1894, Congress authorized their settlement on some Kiowa-Comanche land near Fort Sill in Indian Territory.

In October the remaining 290 Chiricahua climbed out of wagons two miles northeast of the post. They had no livestock and very few clothes or belongings. A number of curious Fort Sill people and Kiowa and Comanche had come to see them. The Apache could not understand their host Indians' sign language. In order to talk, each group brought forward one of their boys who had been trained at Carlisle, the Indian school, and the youngsters conversed in English.

Captain Hugh Scott was in charge of the prisoners. He was an intelligent, humane officer who would help the Apache accomplish much in their new home.

It was too late to make houses, so the tribe made brush wickiups covered with old canvas. In the spring, working under Scott's supervision, the Chiricahua made houses, built fences, and broke ground, where they planted crops and gardens.

Scott let them live in small villages scattered around their part of the reservation. Each had its own headman. Several warriors, including Geronimo, were enlisted as scouts and given uniforms. Naiche, Cochise's son, was given more authority than Geronimo, but Geronimo's exploits made him interesting to whites and he enjoyed this attention. He traveled with Pawnee Bill's Wild West show in 1908 and died of pneumonia in 1909.

The Chiricahua had about fifty able-bodied men. They cut and baled hay, which they sold to the post, and grew melons and vegetables, selling the surplus to local markets. Scott brought in kafir corn, making his Apache the first people in the Southwest to grow it for forage.

Scott also bought cattle for the tribe. This herd became one of the best in the whole region, and sales from it soon were adding a large amount to tribal income. It increased so much that the reservation had to be enlarged. When the Apache stopped living together as a tribe the herd was sold off, bringing $300,000, which was added to tribal money.

The Dutch Reformed Church began mission work among the Chiricahua in 1899. Geronimo joined this church in 1903.

During all this time the tribe was under military supervision and were prisoners of war. Babies born in Florida or Alabama grew up, married, and had children—all prisoners. One by one, the old people died—the warriors and women who had led the U.S. and Mexican armies such a chase.

Nana, who had been almost blind and crippled when he took command of a raid in 1881, died of old age shortly after reaching Fort Sill. Chihuahua, who had surrendered to Crook, saying, "I believe in you and you do not deceive us. You must be our God; I am satisfied with all that you do," died of tuberculosis at the fort.

Naiche and Chato kept pleading for their people to be released, to be permitted to go home. In 1911 it looked as if their bit of Oklahoma land might be taken away. They appealed to the government to give them a home that would always be theirs.

That year the government sent a group of Chiricahua back to New Mexico to decide on a reservation. They had hoped to settle on their old reservation at Canada Alamosa in western New Mexico, but looking at it made them feel sick and robbed.

Overgrazing had desolated the once-lovely valley. Streams were dry and trees chopped down. It was not at all the homeland of which they had dreamed during their long exile.

After a good deal of argument, they decided that of the land available to them, they preferred the Mescalero Apache reservation. Since they could not go back to their former lands, 87 of the remaining 258 Chiricahua decided to stay in Oklahoma, where they had come to feel at home.

In 1913, after twenty-seven years as prisoners of war, they were freed by an act of Congress. They were allowed to stay in Oklahoma or go to New Mexico. That April 171 Chiricahua, mostly of the Central group, got on trains headed for the Mescalero reservation. Naiche and Chato died there, almost back home.

With their share of money from the sale of the fine Apache herd, the 87 Chiricahua who stayed in Oklahoma each bought an 80-acre tract from the Kiowa and Comanche. They built homes on their allotments, and a new town grew up around the Rock Island Railroad. It was called Apache.

Chiricahua in Oklahoma are legal residents of the state. Their children attend local schools. There is no tribal organization. Mostly, they are rural people, farming and raising livestock. Arts and crafts have faded, but the Chiricahua usually have their colorful masked dancers take part in the American Indian Exposition held yearly at Anadarko.

As ritualized art forms die, new individualized ones appear. Allan Houser, grand-nephew of Geronimo, is an outstanding artist with murals in Washington, as well as in Oklahoma.

The Chiricahua who stayed in Oklahoma were mostly the younger ones who had gone to school, grown up in the new region, and had no deep longing for a country they had never seen. About a third of the tribe have intermarried with whites or other tribes, and they live like all the other people in that region.

The Chiricahua who settled on the Mescalero reservation have intermarried with that tribe, and now they are thoroughly mingled. Neither group farms very much, but most families have some cattle. The tribe owns a large herd, and so does the Cattle Growers Association.

Timber cutting has been a major source of income, and in recent years Apache on the Mescalero reservation have gone into the tourist business, opening a tourist center and reviving native arts and crafts for sale.

Some of these Apache still live in brush huts, though the government put up a number of frame houses during the thirties. Many homes do not have indoor plumbing, and heating and cooking are usually done with wood.

The Apache were probably the best all-around fighters ever known. Only overwhelming numbers and unrelenting pursuit finally wore them down. Even the Chiricahua, shipped off as a tribe to distant prisons, remain, though not as a united group.

Poverty and the overshadowing pressures of an alien culture are harder to resist than open enemies, but the spirit with which the Apache survived more than four hundred years of Spanish, Mexican and United States hostility still endures.

FURTHER SUGGESTED READING

Baldwin, Gordon, *The Warrior Apaches*. Tucson, Arizona, Dale King, 1965.

Ball, Eve, *Indeh*. Provo, Utah, Brigham Young University Press, 1980.

Betzinez, Jason, *I Fought With Geronimo*. New York, Bonanza Books, 1959.

Bourke, John, *On the Border with Crook*. Glorieta, New Mexico, Rio Grande Press,1969.

Buchanan, Kimberly Moore, *Apache Women Warriors*. El Paso, Texas Western Press, University of Texas at El Paso, 1986.

Clum, Woodworth, *Apache Agent*. Lincoln, Nebraska, University of Nebraska Press, 1978.

Cruse, Thomas, *Apache Days and After*. Caldwell, Idaho, Caxton Printers, 1941.

Davis, Britton, *The Truth About Geronimo*. New Haven, Connecticut, Yale University Press, 1929.

Debo, Angie, *Geronimo, The Man, His Time, His Place*. Norman, University of Oklahoma Press, 1976.

Goodwin, Grenville, and Basso, Keith H., *Western Apache Raiding and Warfare*. Tucson, Arizona, University of Arizona Press, 1971.

Haley, James L., *Apaches, A History and Culture Portait*. Garden City, New York, Doubleday, 1981.

Lekson, Stephen H., *Nana's Raid*. El Paso, Texas Western Press, University of Texas at El Paso, 1987.

Mails, Thomas E., *The People Called Apache*. Englewood Cliffs, New Jersey, Prentice-Hall, 1974.

Opler, Morris E., *Grenville Goodwin Among the Western Apaches*. Tucson, Arizona, University of Arizona Press, 1973.

Schmitt, Martin, ed., *General George Crook, His Autobiography*. Norman, University of Oklahoma Press, 1960.

Sweeney, Edwin R., *Cochise, Chiricahua Apache Chief*. Norman, University of Oklahoma Press, 1991.

Worcester, Don, *The Apaches, Eagles of The Southwest*. Norman, University of Oklahoma Press, 1979.

Wright, Muriel, *Guide to the Indian Tribes of Oklahoma*. Norman, University of Oklahoma Press, 1951.

THE NAVAJO

The Long Walk

The red lava of Navajo country was believed to be the blood of monsters killed by the Hero Twins, who were sons of Changing Woman. This kindly being had blessed the Navajo at the time of their beginnings and showed them how to live in harmony with even the fierce powers of nature, lightning, wind and storms.

But the Hero Twins could not kill all the monsters. Poverty, Hunger, Dirt and Old Age remained to plague humans. Never did they torment the Navajo so much as during the Long Walk and four terrible years at Bosque Redondo. During those months of death and imprisonment far from their homes, it must have seemed to many Navajo that Changing Woman and all their Holy People were dead and that the Blessing Way no longer had power in this world ruled by white men. At last, though, the Navajo were allowed to trudge back to the canyons where they live today in the Four Corners region, where Colorado, Utah, Arizona and New Mexico meet.

The Navajo are close relatives of the Apache. They descend from Indians such as those living in Alaska and Canada and are known as Athapascans. Before Spaniards brought horses, sheep and cattle to the Southwest, the Navajo lived by hunting, gathering seeds and wild fruit, and growing crops of corn, beans, squash and melons.

After they got sheep and goats from the Spanish, the Navajo depended heavily on them for meat as well as wool. They also became good horsemen, and their swift raids were feared by Spanish settlements and Pueblo Indians.

Borrowing freely from other cultures, the Navajo developed a way of life that was all their own. From the Hopi they got peach trees to plant, and from them and other Pueblo tribes, Navajo learned crafts and

Map 4 Navajo Land

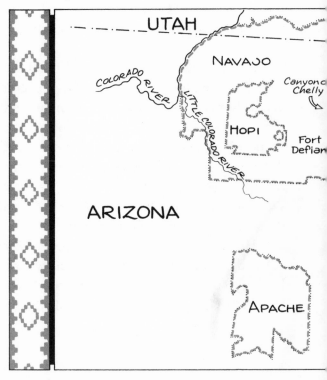

rituals. They also learned from the mounted Plains Indians, and Spaniards brought iron and silversmithing.

Navajo were not roving nomads, though they did move with their herds from winter to summer homes. They lived in family groups, often including relatives; but it was not possible for them to live in large communities because of the scarcity of fuel, grazing, water and game.

When the United States took control of Navajo country in 1846, it found a variety of peoples who had for a long time been raiding one another, taking one another's wives and children as slaves, and somehow finding chances for trade in between fights.

The Navajo had held up their end of the regional strife and were surrounded on all sides by enemies— Ute, Spaniards, Mexicans, Pueblo Indians, and even some Apache. They had fought each other as long as

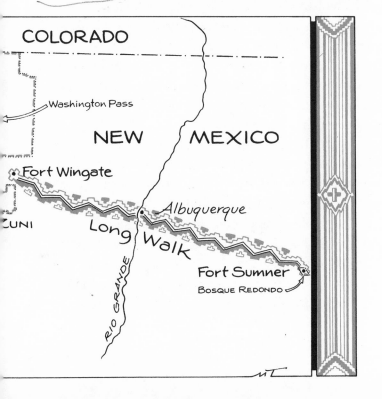

anyone could remember and none of them thought the strange white men marching or riding through the country were going to change things.

Still, in the Treaty of Guadalupe Hidalgo at the end of the Mexican War, the United States had promised to defend the New Mexican settlements and also wished to open the land to American settlers.

Some chiefs and headmen of the Navajo signed treaties with the United States in which they agreed to stay at peace with everyone, but most Navajo never knew about these agreements and would have laughed in bewilderment had they been told. How could marks on paper bring peace among peoples who had warred for centuries?

Besides, a headman could promise for his own little group at most. There was no central authority to make war or peace, no unified council or government.

The Navajo had been fighting the Spanish and then the Mexicans for three hundred years. They pointed out to the Americans that this war was not yet settled just because the United States had ended its own recent war with Mexico. Navajo went on looting slaves and plunder from Rio Grande settlements whenever they had a chance.

After all, they told the U.S. officers, thousands of Navajo were slaves in New Mexican households and others were continually stolen. A Navajo girl or boy five to fifteen years of age could bring up to $200 at auction. Unless the United States could stop this slavery, the Navajo would never stop their own raiding.

For several years U.S. garrisons tried to quiet the Navajo, but they did not have half the success that traders had in stirring the Navajo to raid. These traders made their money from selling ammunition, arms and liquor to the Indians. In order to sell more, they were constantly starting rumors—saying that the United States was going to kill all the Navajo or enslave them or help their old enemies against them.

The conduct of U.S. troops had scarcely done anything to make these traders' tales seem incredible. In 1849 troopers had ridden into the great natural stronghold of Canyon de Chelly, a wildly beautiful system of giant gashes carved by wind and water from the red sandstone. Spaniards had once thought there was a fort deep inside.

Instead, the sandy bottomland was found to be planted with crops and wonderful peach orchards. Navajo hogans were tucked along rock rims, almost invisible to a stranger, and scattered through the thirty mile-long main gorge and its tributaries grazed horses, sheep and goats. It was the heart of Navajo- land and a natural place to refuge from enemies.

Those first troopers pastured their horses on the Navajo grain, and when some headmen came to talk, they fired on them and killed six, including a very old crippled chief, Narbona, who had strongly spoken for peace with the whites.

It was no wonder that in 1851, when Colonel Edwin Sumner marched into the canyon, the Navajo refused to meet with him. As the troopers moved into the vast gorge, Navajo shouted insults from the cliffs and occasionally fired at the dragoons, who were also shooting. Sumner could not pin the Indians down. He had to be content with destroying all the fields and orchards that he saw and then retreated to the new outpost he was building.

This was Fort Defiance at Canyon Bonito. "Handsome" Canyon was a sacred place to the Navajo, who made shrines near the springs and offered turquoise and pretty shells to the spirits there.

Sumner thought, quite rightly, that the Navajo could never be kept peaceful by garrisons stationed far away, but this fort, right in their territory, should prove to them that the United States meant to tame New Mexico.

From the start, soldiers considered Fort Defiance the worst kind of frontier duty. It was 200 miles west of Albuquerque and difficult to supply. Both military and private mail constantly strayed, and the weather went to extremes. Still, the fort served its purpose. Illegal traders and slavers found it hard to get at the Navajo, and as the Indians learned that the U.S. troopers could protect them, they were more inclined to think of peace.

That Christmas of 1851, Colonel Sumner and Territorial Governor James Calhoun met with a number of Navajo headmen. The Navajo were given cloth, brass wire, hoes and spades and other farming implements. They were told that all would be well if they stayed at peace, but if they went raiding, the garrison at Fort Defiance could and would keep them from raising a single patch of corn.

It was a bitter winter. Cold, hungry Navajo drifted into Fort Defiance to test the goodwill of the whites. The post commander collected all the clothing he could find for the Indians and gave them as many hoes and spades as he could find so that crops could be more quickly and easily planted. He saw plainly that the Navajo must be able to live without raiding before they could be expected to give it up. Raiding was not just excitement or vengeance to them but a way of getting enough to live on.

The Navajo returned some New Mexican captives, though two hundred of their own children remained as slaves in New Mexican households. The Indian agent did promise that from now on, all livestock and captives taken by either New Mexicans or Navajo must be returned and the thieves punished.

Comparative peace blessed Navajoland for the first time in decades. Colonel Sumner deepened the friendliness by giving the Navajo more sheep, seeds and farming tools.

But it was too much to hope that peoples who had warred on each other for years would suddenly have no more troubles. The Indians of Laguna Pueblo took over some Navajo lands and used so much of the irrigation water that the Navajo of that region lost a whole year's crop. Traders went on supplying the Navajo with liquor and went on dealing in stolen, cattle and slaves from both sides.

The Indian agent was far away at Jemez, of no use in helping the Navajo with their problems. Though most of the 8,000 to 10,000 tribesmen certainly wanted peace, there were some who meant to live off what they could steal from the New Mexicans. And there were quite a few New Mexicans who kept stealing Navajo sheep and children.

Mounting troubles exploded in May, 1853, when a New Mexican sheepman was murdered and his son and a herder were kidnapped. Only a few renegade Navajo were to blame, but the governor was running for Congressional delegate, and he tried to win the support of the New Mexicans by swearing that unless the five guilty Navajo were surrendered, the whole people would be warred against.

Before such an unfair war could start, the governor was defeated in his attempt to go to Congress. He resigned his office and went back to the States. A new territorial governor was appointed.

This man, David Meriwether, knew the country well from his days as an Indian trader. He had seen that the Navajo were being crowded on the east by Plains tribes, who were being shoved into New Mexico by the thrust of white settlers, and by New Mexican and American settlements, so it was hard for them to be self-supporting.

Governor Meriwether urged vigorous and thorough measures to feed and clothe the Navajo so that they would not need to raid in order to live. If the United States would not do this, the only other way he saw to peace was for the Army to defeat and punish them so mercilessly that they would no longer dare defy the government.

Fortunately, the new Indian agent, Captain Henry Dodge, wanted to use the peaceful method. Even better, he was an experienced soldier and frontiersman. He knew it was useless for an agent to try to help the Navajo from a comfortable office in Jemez or Santa Fe. His first act was to go alone into Navajoland to talk with the people and their headmen.

An official without a big military escort? The Navajo were astounded.

They asked him if he was not afraid to seek them out by himself. Dodge told them he was not afraid because he meant them only good.

If he gave them bad advice or injured them, they were free to kill him. He would never try to be their agent unless he lived among them and knew their problems.

Here was a man the Navajo liked and trusted from the start. The headmen promised him protection from the bad men in their groups. Dodge traveled freely through Canyon de Chelly, saw the orchards and fine corn and herds of sheep and horses, which he estimated at 250,000.

All the way, he made friends. He came back to Santa Fe in September with a delegation of one hundred Navajo. Governor Meriwether spoke to them in a far different manner than other officials had. Hope filled the Navajo as they listened to the good new words.

The governor would listen to the complaints of the Navajo with one ear and to the grievances of whites with the other. Then, he would ponder what both ears heard and make a just decision which then must be obeyed by everyone.

To the headmen he gave medallions. He put a medallion with a larger ribbon around the neck of Zarcillas Largas (Long Earrings) and made him head chief of the whole Navajo Nation, with authority to speak for the entire tribe.

Such an appointment was nonsense, of course. The Navajo did not always heed even their small band's headman. It would have been equally sensible for the Navajo to have picked an Army officer and said that from then on he was the leader of the United States with the right to make agreements for all the people. In spite of this, the meeting was useful.

Many leading men had been at the parley and

liked what Meriwether said. Especially, the Navajo liked and believed in their new agent, who had come so bravely and pleasantly among them.

The next year and a half was most peaceful in Navajo country. Then New Mexicans began to graze sheep on Navajo grass and press the territorial legislature to pass laws permitting this. During the winter of 1853-54 the district court ruled, unbelievably, that there was *no* Indian country in New Mexico!

Stockmen encroached farther on lands already overgrazed by 200,000 Navajo sheep and 60,000 horses. Because of the fantastic ruling of the district court, the Bureau of Indian Affairs had no legal authority to punish traders in slaves and liquor who victimized the Indians.

In spite of these serious setbacks, the Navajo mostly kept the peace and came often to Fort Defiance, where Dodge had placed his agency. He got a blacksmith to teach the Navajo how to forge iron and hired a Mexican silversmith, who probably taught the tribe the craft of silverwork in which they excel today. By spring of 1855 there were eighteen Navajo blacksmiths. With hand bellows and simple Mexican tools, they could make buckles, bridle fittings and much other hardware.

Dodge distributed all the spades, hoes and seed he could get, along with a few plows. By the spring of 1855 the Navajo had about 4,000 acres under cultivation, and the crops were good.

Because of the Fort Defiance garrison, New Mexican slave raids on the Navajo had almost stopped. For the first time, Navajo women and children could tend their flocks without being on the watch for thieves and kidnappers. This was the best period the Navajo ever had.

When Ute from the north came trying to coax them to join in war and raiding on the whites, nearly all the Navajo refused. They told the Ute that the Americans were the best friends they had ever had.

It was also in 1855 when Congress granted power and funds to Governor Meriwether for the making of treaties with Navajo, Ute and Apache. These tribes were to be given permanent ownership of some of the lands they currently lived on; for the regions they gave up to the United States they would be paid in yearly amounts of seed, farm equipment, cloth, and other supplies.

In mid-July the governor traveled to the council site north of Fort Defiance. Agent Dodge had called in the Navajo. Perhaps two thousand of them, representing all but one band which had never had anything to do with whites, gathered in and around a ramada, or brush arbor, of cedar boughs. It was much too small for the great numbers, so many of the armed buckskin-clothed warriors sat on their horses throughout the council.

Tobacco was passed, and after an enjoyable smoke the governor, through interpreters, told the Navajo of the treaty he wished to make with them.

Boundaries, promised the governor, would clearly mark Navajo land from that of their neighbors. There would be no quarrels about trespassing flocks. Besides guaranteeing forever part of their homeland to the tribe, the treaty gave them valuable annuities and undertook to protect them from Ute, New Mexicans, Americans, Pueblo tribes, and anyone else who might appear to trouble them.

The Navajo were given the rest of the day to talk over the proposition, feast, and hold horse races. Next day the actual treaty making began.

Zarcillas Largas resigned as head chief. He said he was too old for the responsibility. A war leader who later would be known as Manuelito became head chief and spoke for the Navajo during, the negotiations, which was all right because all the assembled headmen and warriors agreed to follow his decisions and accept him as their spokesman.

Whites and Navajo had another smoke while a clerk wrote down the treaty. Then Governor Meriwether read it aloud. After each important provision, the Indians were asked if they understood and agreed.

Manuelito raised his people's objections to two major points. First, he said that the reservation granted the Navajo was much smaller than the region they now possessed and that their four sacred mountains were not on the offered reservation. Also, the Navajo had always obtained salt near Zuñi, in an area that would be closed to them.

Governor Meriwether used a map to try to show the Navajo that many of their sacred places were still within their reservation. The 7,000 square miles allotted to them included most of their planting land, probably 125 square miles scattered in small patches along the canyon floor. Anyway, said the governor, the tribe would be paid for the land they gave up in yearly goods that would help them live better.

Manuelito and the headmen talked all this over. They did not want to cede any of their ancestral lands, much less their sacred mountains and other holy places. But they could see all too well that they were hemmed in by other peoples who would gradually push them off much of their territory. At last they consented to the provision.

The next obstacle was the part that bound the Navajo to surrender tribesmen who had committed crimes. The Navajo had sometimes done this to keep the peace, but they did not like it. For one Navajo to surrender another to white justice was dangerous, for it went against all the customs of the tribe and could bring revenge or at least the name traitor. Why could soldiers not come to claim such criminals?

Meriwether answered that Americans usually could not find out who was guilty or where they were and that this clause must be in the treaty. Most reluctantly, the headmen finally agreed, and the treaty was signed.

The Navajo, Meriwether believed, had enough land not only to support themselves but to grow crops they could sell to Fort Defiance. Everyone hoped that peace and prosperity might come at last to that disputed and long-warring country.

Then winter struck the Navajo hard. Bitter, freezing weather began in November, 1855, and lasted through March, 1856. The Rio Grande froze solid enough to be crossed by a horse-drawn wagon. It was 32 degrees below zero on Christmas Day at Fort Defiance, and blizzards killed many horses and sheep.

Some impoverished Navajo went back to their old way of plunder to restock their ranges. They drove off horses, mules and sheep. New Mexicans who were grazing flocks on land the Navajo still considered their own were hit hard.

Late in March a few Navajo ran off 11,000 head of sheep and killed three of their New Mexican herders.

Agent Dodge learned that the thieves were from important Navajo families but were living as outcasts among the Ute. Even so, Manuelito and the headmen refused to hunt down the guilty men and deliver them to punishment.

This would cause civil war, Manuelito said, with the Ute eager to side with the criminals and their supporters against the rest of the tribe. However, to show their desire for justice, the Navajo people would give three servants to replace the herders, as had been their former custom with the New Mexicans, and would replace the stolen sheep. The sheep, argued Manuelito, numbered 4,000, not 11,000. Even so, the Navajo returned more than 1,000 sheep and horses in May and promised to replace the rest, though they would not give up the fugitives.

These attempts at keeping the treaty were broken off when New Mexicans killed two Navajo for no reason, and it was learned that one of the sheepmen claiming big losses in March had not lost a single sheep. The Navajo felt that they would always be blamed and punished, while the New Mexicans escaped justice.

Manuelito defiantly pastured his stock in the fields at Fort Defiance. He said the land had belonged to his people and still did.

Troops had been withdrawn from the fort, so the small garrison could not impress the resentful Navajo. In spite of the chance of provoking a great Indian war, New Mexicans went on grazing flocks on Navajo land. Hot tempers on all sides were ready to explode.

Agent Dodge who understood the Navajo and was liked by them might have been able to smooth over the troubles, but he was killed by Apache in November, 1856, while on a solitary hunt.

To avenge Dodge's killing, three columns of dragoons and infantry went after the Apache from May till September, 1857. It was one of the futile chases that left Indians laughing at whites foolish enough to pursue them in Indian country. Only thirty-two Apache were killed during the whole campaign, and most of the real troublemakers slipped into northern Mexico to raid and plunder—a game they would play for decades to come.

With their friendly agent dead, the Navajo felt surrounded by enemies. The Ute raided them, New Mexicans continued to trespass, and a drought through spring and summer so withered tribal crops that food was scarce even before winter.

This grim prospect grew even worse in early 1858. Some New Mexicans ambushed a party of Navajo and killed two while other New Mexicans and Ute who were on the trail of some Navajo marauders took easy vengeance by killing the first Navajo they met and taking three captives, whom they sold on the auction block for slaves in New Mexican households.

The Navajo raided in reprisal. Then soldiers slaughtered sixty head of Manuelito's horses and cattle because he persisted on grazing them on Fort Defiance pastures. All these troubles festered and came to a bursting point in July, when a Navajo who had quarreled with his woman rode into Fort Defiance and sent an arrow into the back of a servant of Major Thomas Brooks, the post commander.

When the servant died, his murderer was demanded. The Navajo headmen refused to turn him

over and the commander prepared for war. The
Navajo then brought in a body, but it proved to be that
of a Mexican slave shot that morning and not the
killer of Major Brooks' man.

This enraged Brooks. Though he was new to the
region and had no maps of Canyon de Chelly, he
started into the natural fortress with troops. Not
many Navajo were seen and fewer were killed or captured, but much corn was destroyed and thousands of
sheep and horses were taken. By early November
Navajo began coming into Fort Defiance and asking
for peace.

On Christmas Day of 1858 a treaty was made
that could only lead to further bad feeling—a treaty
that the Navajo would have to break in order to survive.

The worst provision of the Bonneville Treaty was
the taking over of the Navajo's best farming and grazing lands, even though the Indian agent pointed out
that this left them with no peaceful way to gain a living.

Other hated terms ruled that the Navajo must
pay New Mexicans for stock losses, though no men-
tion was made about New Mexicans repaying what
they had stolen from the Navajo. All New Mexican
and Pueblo captives were to be released, and all
Navajo would now be held responsible for anything
done by a tribesman. Further, the United States
would make expeditions at any time into Navajo
country and build there any desired forts.

If a treaty had ever been calculated to arouse
anger and provoke its own violation, it was the Bonneville Treaty. In spite of its impossible provisions,
the Navajo tried to obey it through the winter.

They surrendered livestock and captives. Many of

these captives had lived so long among the Navajo that they considered them kinsmen and friends and would not stay with their blood relations.

All the efforts of headmen and those who saw the futility of resistance could not long control a tribe which felt itself so unjustly punished. As spring came, so did raids, plundering and murder of some herdsmen.

Threats, councils and shows of force by the military had little effect. The Navajo said they were being told to give up many times the livestock they had stolen, and besides, what of the animals they had lost? What of their enslaved children and ambushed tribesmen? Why were only the Navajo to suffer?

A few headmen remained friendly to the whites and worked for peace, but this stopped, too, when the new commander of Fort Defiance rashly flogged a Navajo messenger and fired on one of the peaceful headmen who had come to parley.

Full-scale Indian war broke out. The Navajo killed soldiers when they had a chance, waylaid supply wagons, and raided Fort Defiance. Even though the military commander for the region had eighteen hundred fully equipped men, he called for more volunteers and did not march on the Indians. When the U.S. Army took no real action, state militia organized. They battled the Navajo and were often aided by the Ute, who remained eager to war on their ancient enemies.

It took an all-out Navajo attack on Fort Defiance, which nearly led to the fall of the post to jar the Army into motion. After this foray in late April, the U.S. Secretary of War ordered the Army to go after the Navajo and utterly defeat them.

The Army in New Mexico prepared for the

largest, most thorough campaign that territory had ever seen. Six companies of cavalry and nine of infantry were ordered from Utah to New Mexico, and Colonel Edward Canby was put in charge of the Navajo offensive.

Independently, 500 Pueblo Indians and 800 New Mexican militia were getting ready to pursue the Navajo. Colonel Canby did not welcome these "allies" since both groups were age-old foes of the Navajo and would certainly make war with a vindictiveness that could only make the conflict worse.

Still, by mid-October 540 professional soldiers, along with some Ute guides, had collected at Fort Defiance. Canby divided them into three forces. One, led by Major Henry Sibley, marched into Canyon de Chelly. Another large column under Canby would move for the north rim of the canyon to join with Sibley at the west side of the great system of gulches. From there, these two commands together would march toward Black Mesa while a smaller third column would patrol the western end of the canyon to catch Navajo fleeing from the other soldiers.

Sibley and his men pushed up Canyon de Chelly, seeing no Navajo and choking on the fine red dust of the barren rocks because they found no water. After joining Canby's force at the west end of the canyon, the soldiers captured some horses and sheep and killed five Navajo. Almost a month after leaving Fort Defiance, the expedition returned, its horses and men so exhausted that they were of no immediate use.

The great effort had been a complete failure. Canby was angry and disappointed, but he had learned some lessons.

Navajo could fade like shadows, deeper and deeper into their red-rock mazes. There was almost no grass or water for cavalry horses. Before the Navajo could be subdued, overwhelming and merciless pursuit was necessary. Their herds and flocks must be killed or driven away, and their crops destroyed so that they would have no food. Conquering such a swift, elusive and defiant people would be a long, hard, wearing task better done with infantry than by dragoons who, when armed, slowed down their mounts with an average weight of 225 pounds.

As a first step in his new attempt to crush the Navajo, Canby established the new post of Fort Fauntleroy. From there and Fort Defiance, aided by Ute and New Mexican trackers, the Army harassed the Navajo.

Fearing attack, encumbered with the old, the sick, and children, the Navajo had to keep moving in the bitter cold, rarely able to spend more than two nights in the same place. They could not live if they had to stay on the run like this.

By the end of December enough Navajo came in asking for peace to convince Colonel Canby that he could now make a lasting agreement. By mid-February more than two thousand Navajo with about two dozen of their headmen had camped near Fort Fauntleroy to begin talking about the proposed treaty.

Understanding that the Navajo had been hard hit by the long chase, Canby did not make impossible demands for repayment of livestock but tried to start fresh. The treaty ruled that the Navajo would live west of Fort Fauntleroy, keep peace with Pueblo Indians, Ute and New Mexicans, drive out any Navajo thieves, and return any stock taken by them. Also, the tribe was held responsible for what any member might do.

Thirty-two headmen signed the treaty. Canby was so sure that real peace had come that he withdrew all troops from Fort Defiance in April, 1861, and turned it over to the Navajo.

Unfortunately, the Navajo were not the only people involved. As soon as most of the soldiers were transferred south to fight the Apache, New Mexicans began raiding again, killing to take Navajo captives to be sold as slaves throughout the Territory.

It was soon as clear to Canby as it was to the Navajo that many New Mexicans had no intention of changing their old habit of taking slaves, stealing Navajo stock, and running herds and flocks on Navajo land.

Canby vowed to punish all Pueblo Indians and New Mexicans caught in Navajo country, but before he could enforce conditions necessary for peace, the Civil War broke out back in the United States.

All during January and February, 1861, Southern states had been seceding, including New Mexico's neighbor, Texas. Army officers of Southern birth were faced with a terrible conflict of loyalties. Many resigned from the U.S. forces to go home and join the Confederacy. Sibley and Thomas Fauntleroy were among the resigning Southerners in New Mexico. They left Canby with the difficult chore of gathering and reorganizing the remaining troops. By summer they had not been paid for six months, and long droughts had left them few duty-worthy horses.

During this discouraging period, Sibley, now with the Confederacy, got permission to invade New Mexico with the aim of pushing through Arizona to

California, where Southern sympathizers were expected to give the Confederacy a solid foundation throughout the entire Southwest. Sibley and the Confederate government hoped this would break the Union blockade and get European powers to come to the aid of the South.

By summer of 1861 Sibley was pushing for New Mexico with an army of 3,500 Texans. When Canby heard of the invasion, he raised as many volunteers as he could and put one force under famed mountain man and scout Kit Carson, but there were not enough of the poorly trained and equipped men to stop the Texans.

Canby appealed for volunteers from Colorado and California while shifting his meager forces to points that would catch the first brunt of the invaders, who swept up the Rio Grande that summer and fall, capturing Albuquerque and Santa Fe.

But Sibley, with his glorious dreams, would never march into California. Instead, from there and Colorado came two strong forces of volunteers. They completely defeated the Texans at Glorieta Pass in northwestern New Mexico in February, 1862.

The leader of the Californian troops, Brigadier General James Carleton, became the new military commander of New Mexico. No stranger, he had served there against the Navajo and the Apache from 1852 to 1857. Now he found the always-turbulent territory in utter chaos. Without the restraining soldiers who had been busy fighting off Sibley's Texans, New Mexico's warring peoples had fed their old hates and feuds with fresh killings and outrages.

Comanche and Kiowa struck south and east; Navajo raided the west; Mescalero Apache harried the eastern boundaries; and even though the New Mexicans had provoked much of this trouble, Carleton had to stop the Indian raids. From his previous years in New Mexico, he believed the Indians would never really be peaceful till they were absolutely conquered and forced to become farmers.

He planned to defeat the tribes and settle most of them far from their usual homes at Bosque Redondo on the Pecos River in east-central New Mexico, where a new fort, Sumner, would be established to control the conquered Indians and fight off Plains Indians.

Even though the board appointed to investigate the proposed site of Fort Sumner reported that much of the land was likely to suffer heavy spring floods and that the river water and soil contained an unhealthy amount of alkali, Carleton insisted on his plan.

He had studied the location and knew it would be an ideal buffer against Kiowa and Comanche. More important, the region was open and gave no shelter for prisoners who tried to escape. It was a long way from the home of the Apache—and an even longer journey from the slashed red rocks of Navajo land. So erection of the fort proceeded while Canby began his subjection of the tribes.

In the fall of 1862 Kit Carson with New Mexican volunteers reoccupied abandoned Fort Stanton in the middle of Apache country. Two other commands were ordered to close like pincers on the Mescalero Apache and were instructed to take prisoner only women and children.

Five months later the Mescalero were broken. Some escaped to Mexico or Arizona, but most were imprisoned at Bosque Redondo. Here Carleton hoped to turn about four hundred of them into pueblo-like farming Indians.

Next, Carleton turned his attention to the Navajo. He ordered a new fort, Wingate, built close to what is now Grants, New Mexico.

The Navajo, only too aware of what had happened to their Apache relatives, came in to talk peace. Carleton told them he had no faith in their promises and established Fort Canby on the site of old Fort Defiance, while he went on gathering troops to serve under Kit Carson, who had enlisted a hundred Ute to help track their long time enemies.

Even before these authorized forces hit them, the Navajo had greatly suffered from raids by all their old foes, who gladly saw that the U.S. soldiers would not protect the Navajo. Ute prowled the canyons for captives and livestock. New Mexicans eagerly joined in.

Hundreds of Navajo were sold for slaves at the same time the United States was fighting a terrible war with a partial aim of ending the slave system.

Calling themselves "volunteer troops," slave traders combed Navajo country, killing men, stealing stock and carrying women and children off to slavery, which would separate them forever from homeland and family.

Kit Carson honestly believed that these captives would be better off as slaves than they would be at Bosque Redondo, since slaves were usually treated almost like members of the family. Carson even suggested that all captive Navajo be scattered around New Mexico as servants so that they could not survive as a tribe and cause more problems.

Carleton meant to tame the Navajo but did not

want to grind them into oblivion as a people. He ordered Carson to send all prisoners to Santa Fe. From there, they would be resettled on the reservation at Bosque Redondo.

That June of 1863 word was sent to the Navajo that a great war was about to begin against them. Those who did not want to fight and who would consent to live on the reservation on the Pecos must come into Fort Canby or Fort Wingate before July 20. After that date all Navajo remaining outside the forts would be warred on without mercy or ceasing.

Most Navajo had no desire for war but hated the thought of having to live hundreds of miles away, far from their beautiful sacred places, in a land they did not know. Anyway, from the vicious way Ute and New Mexicans had been allowed to kill, plunder and enslave them, the Navajo did not put much faith in the Army's promise of safety if they surrendered.

They did not go to the forts. Late in July, Carson's men went after the Navajo. Within a short time they killed a dozen men, captured twenty women and children, and destroyed 2,000,000 pounds of Navajo grain—nearly all the Indian fields within a day's ride of Fort Canby.

This was a different sort of campaign. Instead of long columns of heavily burdened dragoons and infantry, small groups went out, carrying their rations or packing them on mules, lightly equipped so that they could keep up with the fleet and elusive Navajo. These small units camped near all the springs and water holes to intercept the Navajo when they came for water.

Troops blockaded the mountain passes while

small groups hunted through the canyons. Soldiers got twenty dollars for each good horse or mule turned in to the quartermaster, while Navajo sheep brought a dollar a head.

Some of the hounded Navajo refuged with the few remaining free Mescalero. Some moved west of the Hopi. Others fled north, and some went south to the Arizona Apache. Most Navajo, though, stayed in their native country, even though they began to starve as winter deepened, for their herds had been killed or stolen and their crops burned.

Peace delegations begged for an end to the war, but they were told there was no choice. The Navajo could not stay in their homelands. Either they must surrender and settle on the reservation or stay in their red rocks and die.

In spite of cold and hunger, the Navajo mostly clung stubbornly to their homes. Fewer than two hundred had turned themselves in. In January two commands entered opposite ends of vast Canyon de Chelly to force the rebellious Indians to give up.

Slowly, at first by twos and threes and then in rapidly increasing numbers, the Navajo came into the soldiers' camps and surrendered. They said they would have come in earlier had they not believed it was a war of extermination. Many Navajo, especially babies and young children, had already died of cold and starvation.

Kit Carson told the Navajo that they had ten days to collect their families and come into Fort Canby. Those who did not surrender would be hunted down like wild beasts and slaughtered. Carson went back to Fort Canby to receive the Navajo who came, but he left enough soldiers in Canyon de Chelly to destroy all hogans, fields, and the wonderful peach orchards so beloved by the Indians. Flocks and herds too numerous to be driven easily from the Canyon were to be killed—while their owners starved.

Some Navajo hid deeper in the canyons, living on piñon nuts, roots and the little game they could find, as well as what remained of their herds. Most of the tribe were destitute, however, and in February they began coming into the forts. By early March twenty-five hundred were there and others kept streaming in.

Two thousand of them left Fort Canby early in March with almost 500 of their horses and 3,000 sheep. These were the first to make the heartbreaking journey that would become known as the Long Walk. The Navajo call the four years they were imprisoned at Fort Sumner "Hwelte," a corruption of the Spanish *fuerte*, or fort, and remember it as the worst thing that ever happened to them.

Some Navajo never reached Fort Sumner and the Bosque Redondo. The first travelers were given flour, with no instructions on how to use it. This flour was contaminated by rat droppings and might have caused sickness anyway, but when the Navajo ate it raw or mixed with water, it gave them dysentery.

Many crawled to the roadside and died of exposure or were shot by their guards. While these miserable people were journeying into exile, their tribesmen at the forts were scarcely better off. Blankets and food were in short supply. During one week in March, one hundred twenty-six Navajo died at Forts Canby and Wingate, some from filthy food, others from cold.

There was no refuge for the Navajo. Ute and

P.139

Pueblo Indians went on capturing and enslaving those who were trying to evade the soldiers. In spite of all their fear of the whites and Bosque Redondo, starving, freezing Navajo kept coming into the forts all during that bitter spring.

In April a second large group of about twenty-four hundred Navajo followed their kinsmen to Fort Sumner through heavy snow, which formed heavy drifts along the way. Some of the nearly naked, ailing, hungry people were packed into quartermaster wagons, but most had to walk.

Frozen bodies marked the trail. Dysentery killed many. Guards shot those too sick to march. Frostbite caused the loss of fingers and toes and left festering wounds that often brought gangrenous death.

Other groups followed through the winter of 1863-64, reaching the Bosque Redondo in pitiful condition after the sad and difficult 300-mile march. They had seen their homes, orchards and crops burned, their horses and sheep slaughtered or stolen, their loved ones dead or enslaved.

Ute, Pueblo Indians, and New Mexicans had broken the peace as often as had the Navajo. Why, then, were they the only ones to suffer exile and imprisonment?

Suffer they did, in perhaps the worst conditions endured for any length of time by American Indians forcibly removed from their native grounds.

Carleton probably meant well. He envisioned schools where Navajo children would learn trades and ways of life that would fit them for peaceful, self-supporting lives, and he had irrigation ditches prepared to water the crops the Navajo would plant to feed themselves. But this hardheaded man had disregarded the advice of his officers about alkali in the reservation's water and soil. This foredoomed Carleton's master plan more than anything else, though there were plenty of other reasons for its failure.

Carleton was lumping together more than 400 Mescalero Apache with more than 5,000 Navajo. They had a common language, but neither tribe had ever lived in pueblo-like villages of the sort Carleton wanted, and neither group had the slightest wish to share the tiny area on these dismal plains, far from trees, mountains and good water.

Even if the reservation had been large enough, with pure water and reasonable supplies, the Navajo would have longed for their familiar lands and the daily sight of their sacred mountains.

Added to their grief over dead loved ones and loss of homes and land were constant hunger, disease and being compelled to work under overseers. They were used to freedom. Its loss made them as sick in spirit as ruined food did their bodies.

Carleton had not been able to get even vital food and clothing for the Indians, much less farming implements and supplies. He appealed constantly to the government for enough to keep the Indians alive while he tried to settle the Navajo in a sort of one-story pueblo village.

The Navajo resisted. They had always lived in small bands united by blood relationship. Carleton finally agreed to let them divide into small villages. Over each was a head chief and six subchiefs who were responsible for keeping order in their groups. These headmen in assembly made up a tribal council which was to hold trials for offenders and punish them.

An Army overseer was put in charge of each of the nine Navajo bands. As the representative of the United States, he controlled the lives of those Navajo in his group. He kept the names of men who were able to work, could issue or withhold rations, and had power to punish his charges in almost any way.

Kit Carson, who was reorganizing the tribe, quickly ran into a strange problem. The Navajo had great fear of the dead and always left a hogan where someone had died. In spite of threats and pleading, they would not live in a dwelling where death had struck. After some months of confusion and trouble, Carleton gave up his dream of neat pueblo towns and let the Navajo settle in their familiar family groups.

Carleton's cherished hope of a training school also failed. The building was erected and a priest started classes. At first some Navajo sent their children in hope of getting better food, but when this remained as bad and scarce as ever, the children stayed away from school.

Education for Indians at that time spent much effort in tearing down the Indian religion and trying to convert children to Christianity. The Navajo were not interested in a foreign Holy Land. They had their own hallowed spots and sacred mountains. They did not understand the Christians' all-good male God because the Navajo's sacred beings, like people, were a mixture of good and bad. The Navajo loved and needed Changing Woman, their kind mother deity.

Their religion was born of their fierce beautiful country with its summer heats and winter snows, droughts shattered by torrential thunderstorms. The

Navajo had no need or use for the faith of these white men who had often betrayed them and brought them at last to this place of misery and exile.

In order to feed the Indians at all, Carleton had to put his troops on half rations in March, 1864. At last, cattle and flour were sent from Colorado and saved the Indians long enough for Carleton to push on with his attempt to change Navajo and Apache into pueblo-like Indians.

The Apache had already dug a large irrigation ditch, which was enlarged to water an extra 1,500 acres. At first Carleton thought this would grow enough crops to feed the reservation, but as more Navajo came in till about 8,000 were there, Carleton was terrified. He would have starving Indians on his hands unless something were quickly done.

He ordered the Fort Sumner commander to keep every man, woman and child who could work digging "every moment of the day." At least 3,000 acres must be planted to feed them. They must know that their lives depended on this.

The Navajo dug another great irrigation ditch, 12 feet wide and more than 6 miles long. They did all this in less than a month with only fifty spades and, besides, dug 15 miles of small canals to bring water into their parched fields.

Much of the land had to be cleared, a job now taking bulldozers. The smallest mesquite tree has a fantastic network of roots to suck water from deep levels. Ripping one up is backbreaking labor even with hoes, spades, picks and axes. The Navajo had few tools. Most used their bleeding fingers to scratch the dirt from the roots and then hacked tough fibers out with rocks and sticks.

With slow tedious labor, Navajo cleared 3,000 acres and planted corn, squash, melons and beans. Meanwhile, food was desperately needed, and Indian officials moved slowly in spite of Carleton's appeals and warnings.

"We can feed them cheaper than we can fight them," he wrote the Adjutant General. But the Bureau of Indian Affairs had no money with which to feed suddenly 8,000 Navajo. Many officials had been against Carleton's plan from the start and were not going to help it succeed, even if its collapse meant death and starvation for all the Indians.

New Mexico's Superintendency for Indian Affairs could not cope with Carleton's huge undertaking. Superintendent Michael Steck visited Bosque Redondo and told high officials in the Indian Office that the reservation was barely large enough for the Mescalero Apache, allowing 12 acres of cropland for each family. It was madness to hope to support the entire tribe of 10,000 Navajo with their horses and sheep on the 40 square miles of arid land. Steck urged that the Navajo be given a reservation back in their own country.

Carleton was furious at this interference with his pet project for solving the territory's Indian woes. He pointed out that his idea had been endorsed by the late Superintendent for Indian Affairs, the legislature, and Kit Carson. It is possible that Carleton hoped to find gold or silver in the Navajo land and for this reason wanted to keep them away; but he also dreamed of bringing them peace, and it is one of the bitter ironies of Indian history that he brought them only misery.

The Bureau of Indian Affairs within the Department of the Interior refused to take responsibility for the Navajo and left them to the Army. Superintendent Steck fought against making the Apache share the small reservation with the Navajo, and back in the West, Navajo raids made some settlers complain that the most warlike Navajo had never been caught and were still hiding in their winding canyons. Some of these raids were the work of marauding New Mexicans and others, but there was little doubt that several hundred tough battle-ready Navajo remained deep in their wilderness.

This added weight to Steck's argument that the Navajo could never entirely be forced to the Pecos. Even if they were, they could not be fed. It cost $50,000 monthly to feed the 6,000 Navajo still living on the reservation. This was done on short rations of less than a pound of food a day for each person. Many children were dying of malnutrition. It was useless to try to civilize people who were starving.

In April, 1864, the commander of Fort Sumner called the headmen to council. He told them the meat ration could be slightly increased. If they used every scrap of food and worked hard at putting in crops, their people would soon live comfortably, with adequate food and clothing.

The headmen went back to their bands with this encouraging message. It was hard in this flat land, but if they worked the fields with patience, there would be food. And perhaps—perhaps if they could stay alive —they might one day go back to their beloved canyons.

That summer, 3,000 acres of crops were maturing. These had been put in without implements by a weakened, heartsick people driven by overseers. Still, as the Navajo watched corn tassel, melons ripen and beans grow, it must have seemed worth all their labor. They began to feel more hopeful of surviving on the reservation.

But as the corn swelled, cutworms attacked, devouring budding ears of ripening corn, destroying the work of months, and raising the dread of starvation. The disappointed, frightened Navajo reminded themselves that the wheat flourished. That might sustain them through the winter.

This wheat, so watchfully cherished, was almost ready to harvest in late October when severe storms flattened the heavy stalks to the ground. Only half the crop could be saved. To make the food problem even more desperate, storms had ruined the crops of neighboring farmers, so these could not be bought to tide the Indians over.

Rations were cut. Commanders at Forts Wingate and Canby were ordered not to send more Navajo to the Bosque Redondo till further notice. Those who were there began to slip away.

In spite of hard work and patience, they were going hungry, watching their children starve. They might as well die on their way home as perish in the alkaline dust of the Pecos.

Carleton, far from deciding his resettlement plan was futile, commanded irrigation ditches enlarged, new fields cleared, and every bit of possible land plowed in readiness for early planting.

If 9,000 acres were planted, this should supply all the Indians and garrison of Fort Sumner. Corn must not again be so largely counted on. Three thousand acres would be planted to early maturing wheat, and beans could then grow on the same land during summer months.

This seemed a good arrangement. All that was wrong with Carleton's schemes was that he expected crops to grow in soil and water that would poison them. He was a soldier used to being obeyed; he did not understand that the earth could not be commanded.

Apart from the worst problem of food, fuel was almost gone, and both soldiers and Indians had to travel miles in search of wood. Again defying the desert nature of the Pecos country, Carleton ordered Fort Sumner's commander to plant 5,000 trees which would, in time, supply plenty of fuel.

Some New Mexican newspapers had at first supported the reservation plan, but by now they were attacking it, pointing to the repeated disasters at Bosque Redondo, the staggering cost of feeding the Indians on even short rations, and raids by the Navajo who were still hiding out in their red canyons.

Carleton persisted in his dream, which was the Indians' nightmare. In January, 1865, supplies bought with $100,000 appropriated by the U.S. Congress finally arrived. Clothing, blankets, tools and other supplies were given out, and 4,000 sheep were turned out to graze and fatten to make food for the famished people.

Even these late and meager supplies were a swindle. Much of the money had been spent on unnecessary supplies such as leather, which was cheaply and easily on hand at the fort. Ridiculous prices had been paid for things like blankets, often three times as much as articles of better quality cost.

Carleton sent in a report showing that the $100,000 had bought only one-half to one-third of what it should have. This angered officials responsible for the purchases, and the following accusations and countercharges ended the small amount of cooperation that remained between the military and Bureau of Indian Affairs people in New Mexico.

Instead of working together for the good of the Indians, these two groups fought for control while the state of the Indians was as that of a bone caught between two big dogs.

The agent for the Mescalero Apache had never wanted Navajo settled with his people. He had always reported every bad thing he could about the Army's management of the Navajo, though he was far from admirable himself.

He was running a large flock of his own sheep on scarce reservation graze, and he either was not trying to get the Apache to farm or was failing miserably. Only one hundred and sixty acres were under cultivation, and most of these had been planted by hired Mexican labor. Army people at Fort Sumner kept watch on this agent, Lorenzo Labadie, caught him in fraud and theft, and brought on trial two Army officers who had sold him Army cattle and supplies.

These officers were found guilty and dismissed from the service. Since Labadie was a civilian, the Army could only make him leave the reservation.

He did, simply moving his agency beyond military borders. Here he continued in his office, far from the Apache he was paid to help. They probably did not miss him. He had never been useful, and like the Navajo, the Apache were sick of the reservation.

Mescalero Apache were not farming Indians like the Navajo or some of their own Arizona relatives.

They thought growing crops was fit only for despised tame Indians. It was said a hoe hadn't been made that would fit an Apache's hand. Living near the plains, Mescalero were hunters, travelers and raiders. Their habits decreed that they could not abruptly turn into farmers at Bosque Redondo, and the flood of Navajo doomed that hope completely.

Added to dislike of farming and the reservation was real fear of the Navajo. In times past, these tribes had frequently warred on each other. Now the Mescalero were outnumbered twenty to one, and the Navajo were good at remembering past feuds and troubles. Fort Sumner's garrison prevented bloodshed, but Mescalero were convinced they were in danger if they stayed penned up with their enemies on the tiny reservation.

In November, 1865, all Mescalero, except nine aged and feeble ones, vanished suddenly from the Bosque Redondo, fading into their old range to the south. This proved what critics had argued all along: Navajo and Apache could not live together.

Earlier in that year, in the same January that brought the tardy supplies to the Navajo, every Navajo able to work had been put to clearing land, digging irrigation channels, and preparing to plant 6,000 acres of crops.

By spring 3,000 acres were in corn, 1,000 in wheat, and the remaining 2,000 acres were planted with pumpkins, melons, beans, peas and squash.

The post commander was sure the crops would feed the Navajo well. Even figuring a low yield per acre, there should be 9,000,000 pounds, enough to give each Indian 3 pounds of food a day.

But the cutworm hatched again in the damp silk of young ears of ripening corn. The Navajo watched in helpless despair. The corn crop was heartbreakingly small, so was the wheat, and the other crops yielded far below reasonable expectation. Only 500,000 pounds of the 9,000,000 needed came from the fields cleared by such labor, watered by painfully dug ditches, and tended with great hope.

By now the Navajo believed crops would not grow here. No matter how hard they worked, alkaline water poisoned the earth and stunted any crop that worms and storms spared. Even though the Navajo hated the reservation, they had desperately tried to live there, but it was no use. There would never be enough food or blankets or clothing, and all the time they longed for their beautiful wild canyon home.

Besides all this, Comanche-Kiowa raids were common by the spring of 1865. They considered the Pecos region part of their vast range and did not like to find a reservation barring their way into New Mexico, where, for a long time, they had traded with the New Mexicans and warred on the Navajo.

To form such a barrier had been a prime reason for Carleton's locating the reservation at Bosque Redondo. Now the unlucky Navajo drew the lightning of Comanche raids. These began with small groups of a dozen or so warriors but shortly grew into attacks by hundreds of Comanche, who swooped in to kill any Navajo they found and run off their horses.

Haunted by this peril, as well as by hunger, homesickness, dysentery, malaria, and venereal disease, which may not have begun at the Bosque but certainly multiplied there, more and more Navajo began to steal away, preferring death on the way home to what amounted to life in a filthy, dangerous concentration camp.

Carleton put out more guards and patrols, but many Navajo evaded capture and got back to their homes. On their way they killed and ate New Mexican livestock. Complaints from the owners added to Carleton's headaches.

By June of 1865 more than a thousand Navajo had escaped. Troops and volunteers were ordered out to try to stop the runaways before they got west of the Rio Grande. Navajo still on the reservation were told that the fugitives who did not return to the Bosque would be exterminated and that many had already been killed. Any Navajo found off the reservation without a pass would die. In spite of these warnings, more Navajo slipped away each day. The reservation was so intolerable that they would rather die than stay there.

Now that the Civil War was over, the nation began to notice the increasing Indian troubles. Some friends of the Indians insisted that most of these wars and problems resulted from crimes and trespassing of white men, broken treaties and bad faith. A Congressional committee was formed to investigate the condition of all United States Indians.

Much of this massive task had to be done by letters and reports of Army officers, Indian agents and superintendents. In spite of a good deal of covering up, there were enough honest, angry Bureau of Indian Affairs men and Army officers to prove that in most cases whites had driven the Indians into retaliation and war.

It took investigators only a brief hearing in Santa Fe and a shorter look at the Fort Sumner reservation to learn how unjustly the Navajo had been treated. True, they were raiders, but so were all their enemies who had hunted and enslaved them, often with the help of U.S. officials. Anyway, whatever had happened in the past, present facts were shocking and indisputable.

Bosque Redondo was a prison camp full of sick, starving people. Crops could not flourish in such alkaline soil. In late 1865 a special agent, Julius Graves, was sent to talk with the Navajo and make a full report to the Congressional committee.

Agent Graves told the assembled headmen that the government wanted them to be well fed and comfortable. What did they think would be good for their tribe?

The headmen pleaded for return to their old home. They promised that if only they could go there, they would be peaceable.

"Chain the eagle to the ground," one Navajo told Graves. "He will strive to gain his freedom, and though he fails, he will lift his head and look up at the sky which is his home. We want to return to our mountains and plains. . . ."

Agent Graves reported Navajo feelings to the committee, along with his own conviction that if the Navajo were compelled to stay on the reservation either the Army or Bureau of Indian Affairs must be solely responsible and must be given adequate means to care properly for the tribe.

In spite of this advice, a new agent was sent to the Navajo in 1866. Fortunately this man, Theodore

Dodd, was an ex-military man and acceptable to Carleton. With great energy, Dodd cut through red tape and personally got authorization from Washington to buy supplies. He ordered farming implements, clothing, tools, sheep shears, wool cards and other necessities in St. Louis, where he arranged for their transportation to Fort Sumner.

A man of intelligence and vigor, Dodd truly wanted to help the Navajo, but there was nothing he could do about the alkali in the water and soil. In 1866, for the third bitter time, the land proved that it would not feed those who worked it with such effort and pain.

Dodd decided to give up the big fields and let each band plant and tend small plots as they had done back in their own country. But it was too late for this man of goodwill to hearten the Navajo. They were weak and sick, always hungry, always homesick. Why should they plant crops that would only blight or wither?

They worked their plots that spring of 1867 but under threat of bayonets. Drought shrank the Pecos to a dribble. The few surviving crops were blasted by hail storms.

It was a cursed land, and use had made it even grimmer and more desolate. All mesquite, cedar and cottonwood near the fort had been used. The Navajo traveled 20 miles hunting mesquite roots for fuel while the garrison sent wagons and teams 40 and 50 miles away in search of wood.

While this was happening at Fort Sumner, officials in Washington were studying the reservation and its cost. The New Mexican Territorial Assembly in January, 1866, had sent a document to President

Andrew Johnson asking that Carleton be replaced by a more effective commander. He was transferred in September, and on the last day of 1866 control of the Navajo passed from the Army to the Bureau of Indian Affairs.

This was done without clear directions. Worse, Congress had not appropriated enough money to care for the Navajo, who suffered from cold, hunger and Comanche raids while far away the men who controlled their lives struggled with red tape.

Dodd was trying to cope with the reservation till someone else took charge. He wrote officials that the government must either feed the Navajo decently or turn them loose.

Finally, when the Department of the Interior announced that it would become responsible for the Navajo in September, it was learned that the commander of Fort Sumner had never been formally ordered to surrender control of the reservation to Dodd. The Army was insisting on a final inspection and report on the reservation.

They got it from a Lieutenant R. McDonald, who told of wretched conditions and urged that the tribe be moved where wood, grass and water were plentiful.

General Sherman thought the Navajo should be sent to Oklahoma. Luckily for the Navajo, both the Commissioner of Indian Affairs and the Secretary of the Interior favored sending the Navajo back to their home country.

Late in October, full control of the Navajo was given to the Bureau of Indian Affairs in the person of Agent Dodd. He suggested that a commission go at once to the old Navajo land and select a reservation with plenty of wood, water and cropland.

General William Sherman and Colonel Samuel Tappan came to Fort Sumner in May, 1868, determined that the Navajo should go to Oklahoma. But the Navajo pleaded to go back to their old home, and Barboncito, one of the leaders, took his knife from his moccasin and told the white officers that he wished to be killed if his people could not return to their own land.

There was power in Barboncito's speaking, for he held beneath his tongue a bit of turquoise brushed with pollen. Before the parley, some of the men had caught a coyote and sprinkled pollen on him. Then they rubbed the turquoise through his fur so that this "live" pollen would carry with it the wisdom and craftiness of the animal.

Barboncito and the others pleaded so strongly that even Sherman relented. He made a new treaty with the Navajo on June 1, 1868. The Navajo promised to live at peace on a reservation of 5,000 square miles—3,500,000 acres out of the 23,000,000 they had owned. The United States was to maintain a carpenter and blacksmith shop, a school, chapel, and agency on the reservation. For ten years, each Navajo was to get clothing, goods and supplies worth no more than $5, and each Navajo who farmed or worked with tools should have a $10 bonus.

The impoverished tribe who had before Fort Sumner owned 250,000 sheep now had fewer than 1,000. Of 60,000 horses, only 1,500 were left. The United States allowed $150,000 to give the tribe a new start and also supplied them with 15,000 sheep and goats and 500 head of cattle.

At dawn on June 18 the Navajo started home. Their long column stretched 10 miles, and they could travel no more than 12 miles a day. Four companies of cavalry guarded them. Nearly every family had left dead at Fort Sumner, and many were sick and weak.

Still, they were happy. They were going home, to their red rocks and Four Sacred Mountains which marked, for the Navajo, the center of the world and the place where mankind had been created.

When they reached Fort Defiance, some fell to their home earth as if to embrace it and wept. And the old men had a ram tied to a tree where he could be seen by everyone as he vainly tried to butt his way to freedom. Just as foolish and useless, warned the headmen, was it to try to defy the whites. The Navajo had battled enemies on all sides for centuries, but after the Bosque Redondo they wished only to live in their own country and be at peace.

There were good agents and bad; good crops and ruined crops. The destroyed peach orchards grew up again from their old roots better than ever. Herds and flocks multiplied.

Schools were set up, but even after the compulsory education law of 1887, few children attended regularly. It was really not till World War II, when many young Navajo served in the military and had to live outside the reservation, that a strong desire for education grew within the tribe. In 1966 about one-third of the tribe were in schools of one kind or another, ranging from Head Start classes to college.

In 1884 the reservation was extended west to give the growing tribe an additional 8,000 square miles. In the five years since their return from Fort Sumner, the Navajo increased from about 10,000 to 17,000. Today they number over 200,000 and are the largest tribe in the United States.

Traders, who encouraged weaving and silver-smithing, probably did more than the agents to help the Navajo become self-supporting. By about 1890 few rugs were woven in the old laborious way from hand-carded wool dyed with vegetable colors. Navajo women used brilliantly dyed wools imported from the East and could thus triple or quadruple their valuable rugs. These brought income to keep a family going when crops failed, as did the beautiful silver and turquoise jewelry designed by the men.

Aside from giving up raiding, the Navajo way of life did not have to change radically or all at once. Their old habits of farming and sheep raising did not have to end. In spite of the four shattering years at Bosque Redondo, the Navajo had kept their religion, language and identity as a people.

Helping them, too, was their old ability to adapt. They had learned weaving and agriculture from Pueblo Indians, smithing, herding and probably sewing from New Mexicans. From the white man they learned how to use their skills to make things that could be sold, and they began to learn better ways of agriculture and sheep raising.

New industries have developed in Navajo country: electric power production, oil, gas, manufacturing, coal mining and helium and uranium processing. There is simply not enough land to support the people through agriculture and sheep. New ways of earning a living must be found.

The Navajo eagerly set up a number of self-help programs through President Lyndon Johnson's OEO

War on Poverty. They also take a strong interest in council elections. More and more young Navajo go to school or jobs beyond the reservation, and as they become able to move back and forth between the two worlds, much of the hopelessness of belonging to a culture surrounded by a stronger alien one will vanish.

Few Navajo care to live long in the strange rootless world of the whites. Overcrowded on the reservation, some have moved in groups to form new farming communities on unoccupied lands. More study to become teachers, nurses and other professionals. Tourism is being recognized as income-producing.

More than any other tribe, the Navajo have retained their ancient ways while learning to live with the white man. Finally, it is occurring to both that our white society has lessons to learn from the Indians on how to feel a part of the natural world and how to live in families and groups that give the individual a sense of purpose beyond his own achievements and private life.

FURTHER SUGGESTED READING

Bailey, Lynn, *Bosque Redondo.* Pasadena, California, Socio-Technical Publications, 1970.

—— *The Long Walk.* Pasadena, California, Socio-Technical Publications, 1964.

Bennett, Kay and Russ, *A Navajo Saga.* San Antonio, Texas, The Naylor Company, 1969.

Dyk, Walter, recorder, and Left Handed, *Son of Old Man Hat: A Navaho Autobiograhy.* Lincoln, University of Nebraska Press, 1967.

Haile, Father Berard O.F.M., *Navajo Coyote Tales*. Tucson, University of Oklahoma, 1984.

Luckert, Karl W., *Navajo Mountain and Rainbow Bridge Religion*. Tucson, University of Arizona Press, 1977.

Underhill, Ruth, *The Navajos*. Norman, University of Oklahoma Press, 1956.

Wellman, Paul I., *Death in the Desert: The Fifty Years' War for the Great Southwest*. Lincoln, University of Nebraska Press, 1987.

Yazzie, Ethelou, *Navajo History*. Many Farms, AZ, Navajo Community College Press, 1971.

THE CHEROKEE

The Trail of Tears

From 1785 to 1902 the Cherokee signed twenty-five treaties with white men. Eighteen of these gave up tribal lands!

At the coming of the whites, the Cherokee lived in Georgia, the Carolinas and Tennessee. British traders married into the tribe from the beginning, and these mixed-blood families tended to become prosperous and powerful, owning plantations and large herds of cattle. During the French and Indian War, the Cherokee aided the British till the arrogance of a few British officers and murder of some tribesmen provoked the tribe into warring against them. Upon ending the war with France, English leaders made peace with the Southern tribes, including the Cherokee, and signed a treaty of peace and friendship.

What this really meant was that the Cherokee and other Indians should stay friendly and peaceful while giving up more and more of their land. This all began in 1721, when the Cherokee ceded some South

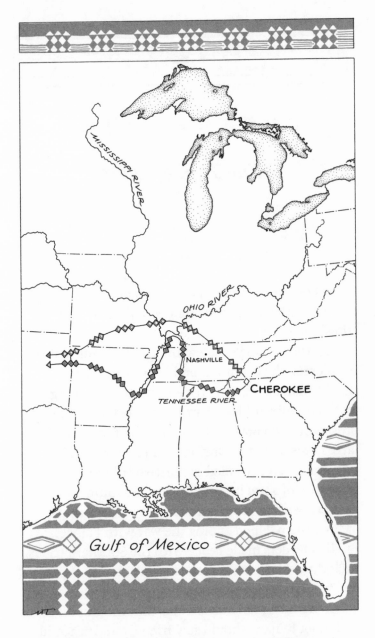

Map 5 Cherokee Migration Routes

Carolina land to the whites of Charleston. Even without cession, white frontiersmen poured into the fertile region. After the Revolutionary War, the Cherokee lost the rest of their South and North Carolina holdings and most of Tennessee because they had fought for the British.

What wasn't taken by treaty was taken by squatters. When the Cherokee protested, George Washington wrote to them in 1794: "More than ten thousand white people are seated on these lands and they cannot be removed. . . ."

Apparently the Indians could be, even though they were far more civilized than most of the whites crowding in. When the British started coming among them, the Cherokee lived in separate clay dwellings around a Town House where village affairs were handled. Fields of corn, potatoes and beans stretched away from the town.

The men were good hunters but helped with the farming. Hogs and poultry were raised even before the American Revolution, and most families owned horses. After the United States began dealing with them, it furnished the Cherokee with spinning wheels, looms and farming implements, which quickly put the Cherokee on a domestic and agricultural level with the whites. By 1820 spinning and weaving were important Cherokee industries.

While many frontier whites were illiterate, most Cherokee could read both their own language and English because of a mixed-blood named Sequoyah. Reared in the old tribal way, with no schooling or knowledge of English, he worked for many years to devise an "alphabet" or syllabary of eighty-five characters that represented combination vowel and consonant sounds of Cherokee.

The Cherokee were thrilled by this. By 1822 they were reading and writing in their own language, the first Indians to be able to do so.

They also had the first written law, adopted by the Cherokee Nation's council in 1808. This was based on the U.S. Constitution and authored by Charles Hicks, a mixed-blood friend of Sequoyah's.

Hicks also persuaded his people to let missionaries set up churches and schools in Cherokee lands. The first mission school opened in 1801, and others followed fast. Circuit-riding Methodist ministers began holding regular services in 1822, and the active Baptists won many converts.

In 1798 the United States signed the Treaty of Tellico with thirty-nine Cherokee leaders, swearing that the remaining 43,000 square miles of tribal land should belong to the Cherokee "forever." Twenty-one years later these lands shrank to one-third, and the United States pressured the Cherokee into allowing roads to cross their land. Roads inevitably brought in settlers.

The ink was scarcely dry on the Treaty of Tellico when, in 1802, as a condition for Georgia's agreeing to cede to the United States her unsettled western region (now Alabama and Mississippi), the United States promised to move all Indians from Georgia "as soon as it could be done peacefully and upon favorable terms."

Thomas Jefferson's proposal for solving the Indian question was to move all the Eastern Indians into Louisiana Purchase lands. It was clear to many troubled Cherokee that their ability to adopt the white man's ways would not save them. They were going to be crowded out of their homes.

By 1815 nearly 3,000 Cherokee had migrated to what later became Arkansas. Two years later about 4,000 ceded their Eastern lands in return for "permanent" grants in Arkansas.

Tribal law decreed death to any Cherokee who proposed to sell or exchange tribal land. Under this law, Chief Doublehead of the Chickamauga branch of the Cherokee was executed by a committee headed by Major John Ridge. Ridge, who had fought with valor under Andrew Jackson, used his military rank as a first name, and we will follow this usage to distinguish him from his son, John Rollin Ridge.

This killing and this law would bring on a blood feud that would divide the Cherokee long after they reached Indian Territory. Meanwhile, relentless pressure on all Cherokee continued.

In 1828 those Cherokee living in Arkansas were persuaded to exchange their Arkansas holdings for 7,000,000 acres farther west, including much of what is now northeastern Oklahoma. These western Cherokee were also to have a permanent outlet to the West, which would later be popularly called the Cherokee Strip.

The year 1828 was a fateful one for the Cherokee. The *Cherokee Phoenix*, a national newspaper edited by Elias Boudinot and printed in both Cherokee and English, was launched. John Ross was elected principal chief, beginning his long trying years as leader of his people. Gold was discovered in Cherokee lands, impelling Georgia to press ruthlessly for the United

States to carry out removal of the Cherokee as agreed in the Georgia Compact of 1802. Finding gold in one's backyard did not mean fortune to the Indians, but disaster, especially when 1828 also brought the election of Andrew Jackson as President.

The Cherokee had good reason to hope Jackson would help them. Principal Chief John Ross had helped Jackson defeat the raiding "Red Stick" Creeks. Another Cherokee, Junaluska, had saved Jackson's life at the Battle of Horseshoe Bend during the Creek War of 1814, and it was for valor in these battles that Jackson had promoted Ridge to the rank of major.

When Jackson made his inaugural address in 1829, his words sounded comforting. "It will be my sincere and constant desire, to observe towards the Indian tribes within our limits, a just and liberal policy; and to give that humane and considerate attention to their rights and their wants, which are consistent with the habits of our government, and the feelings of our people."

In spite of these promises, Jackson needed the support of land-hungry frontiersmen and was determined that the Indians should all go west—Cherokee, Creek, Seminole, Choctaw and Chickasaw, the Five Civilized Tribes. Except for a few Seminole and Cherokee who managed to elude capture and hide out in their home regions, these tribes were forced to Indian Territory, now Oklahoma, but the Cherokee suffered most on the Trail of Tears.

Confident that President Jackson would support it, Georgia put the Cherokee Nation under state law in 1828. Cherokee were arrested and jailed on the slightest excuse, whites who committed crimes against the Indians were not punished, and in every way possible the Cherokee were persecuted in an effort to make them give up their land. They were even forbidden to mine gold on their own property!

The Cherokee, who had a legal system, written constitution and laws, good schools, churches, a postal service and bilingual national newspaper which nearly every Cherokee could read, were not going to be able to live in their home country once this was desired by "civilized" white people!

Elias Boudinot, nephew of Major Ridge and like his cousin, John Ridge, married to a beautiful, cultured white girl of good family, wrote in the *Cherokee Phoenix* that if the United States did not protect the Cherokee from Georgia, the tribe could have "no confidence left that the United States will be more just and faithful toward us in the barren prairies of the west than here on the soil inherited from the Great Author of our existence."

There is tragic irony in the way that refined, educated Cherokee, often Christians and owners of large plantations, went to Washington to plead with men who were almost illiterate to let the Cherokee stay in their homes.

Whites often justified wars on Indians as being against savage heathen foes. The Cherokee were neither, nor were they a danger to the whites. Pure land greed alone was the cause for their being cruelly driven from their beloved country.

To justify their expulsion, the Cherokee were pictured as primitives. One Georgia Congressman who had claimed they lived on roots, herbs and disgusting reptiles was embarrassed during one Washington dinner when he was seated near several Cherokee delegates who kept calling for "more of those roots" instead of asking for potatoes and who remarked jokingly that Indians were very fond of roots. A culture that tries to judge another will find itself caught in laughable inconsistencies.

In 1830 the Removal Bill passed narrowly. It did not call for forced moving by the Cherokee but provided money and authority to negotiate with the tribes. The Cherokee cause was defended by many important whites, Noah Webster, John Adams, Sam Houston, who was an adopted Cherokee, and even that first ranking frontiersman Davy Crockett. But Jackson and his supporters were determined that the Indians must all move, west, and the federal government continued to allow Georgia to harass the Cherokee.

Soon Georgia indicted and imprisoned a missionary, Samuel Worcester, who had remained to work among the Cherokee without getting a permit or taking an oath of allegiance to the state. His suit was appealed to the Supreme Court, which in 1832 ruled in his favor and pronounced all Georgia legislation concerning the Cherokee unconstitutional, null and void.

This is when President Jackson remarked scornfully, "John Marshall has made his decision; let him enforce it now if he can!" Marshall, Chief Justice of the Court, could not do this, as Jackson well knew.

A system like that of the United States, which depends on the executive power to enforce legislative and judicial decisions, cannot work properly when the executive branch cannot or will not enforce laws. Jackson deserved to be impeached, of course, but he was a hero to most of the country, and his will reflected its mood. The Indians had to go.

Georgia placed the Cherokee under martial law and forbade them to assemble, so their government had to be conducted from Alabama. All this time the federal government threatened and persuaded, even trying to bribe Cherokee leaders. Gradually, some of the Cherokee, especially the mixed-bloods, came to believe that futher resistance could only bring more trouble to their people and that it was best to make a treaty on the most favorable terms they could get.

The leaders of this Treaty Party were Major Ridge, his son John, and two of Major Ridge's nephews, Elias Boudinot and Stand Watie, who would later become a brigadier general in the Confederate Army. Principal Chief John Ross and an overwhelming majority of the Cherokee refused to negotiate. Both sides sent rival delegations to Washington. The whites had succeeded in splitting the Cherokee Nation and dividing its leadership, all fine men and patriots who desired good for their people.

On December 29, 1835, Major Ridge, his son, nephews, and others of the treaty party signed the Treaty of New Echota. Only about 500 Cherokee attended out of 17,000, but the United States ratified this agreement, which ceded the last Eastern holdings of the Cherokee. Ratification was by a single vote after a bitter struggle, for everyone knew most Cherokee had not agreed to the treaty.

Chief Ross sent the government a petition signed by almost 16,000 of the 17,000 Cherokee involved. This repudiated the treaty and declared that the Cherokee were not bound by it since it "was made by a few unauthorized individuals and the Nation is not a party in it."

Major Ridge must have remembered how long ago he had helped kill Doublehead for signing away Cherokee land. Even fresher was the memory of how he and his son John had been active in having put down in writing the law providing death for those who sold land without authorization of the tribal council. John Ridge, in fact, wrote to a friend that when he signed the Treaty of New Echota, he knew he was signing away his life, but that he did it in the belief that this might save his people from suffering.

The treaty ceded all Eastern Cherokee lands to the United States in return for joint interest in the Indian Territory lands granted to the Western Cherokee in exchange for their Arkansas holdings. A tract of 800,000 acres called the Neutral Land in what is now southeastern Kansas was added. The treaty bound all Cherokee to move west within two years, and the United States was to pay the cost of the immigration and living expenses for one year after the Cherokee reached their new country. The Cherokee could sell their homes, barns and livestock for money paid directly to each owner.

The Cherokee gave up 8,000,000 acres of land for about 50 cents an acre. Shortly after the treaty was ratified, land speculators were selling 40-acre tracts in the gold region for up to $30,000.

Soon after signing the treaty, Major Ridge and about 600 supporters left for Indian Territory, hoping their tribesmen would soon follow. They were well received by the Western Cherokee, or Old Settlers, and by the end of 1837 John Ridge, Boudinot, and others of the Treaty Party had settled in fertile country near the Arkansas-Missouri border.

They built homes and barns, cleared brush, and planted. The Ridges opened a general store and John Ridge built a school. Boudinot sought out the Reverend Mr. Worcester, the staunch missionary who had gone to jail for helping the Cherokee and who had come to live with them in this new land.

The two began translating into Cherokee books, almanacs and other useful volumes. It did not take long for members of the Treaty Party to become valued and at home in Indian Territory. Many Western Cherokee did not approve of the Treaty of New Echota, but they did not look on the Ridges as traitors who had forfeited their lives. Meanwhile, the great majority of the Eastern Cherokee, about 15,000 people, made no preparations for moving as May 1838, the deadline for leaving Georgia, approached. They hoped that Chief John Ross would somehow manage to preserve their homes. That spring, as always, they planted their fields. In spite of persecution from Georgians, this was their land, where their parents were buried, and many would have preferred death to leaving it.

Most of these people were full bloods. Since many of the Treaty Party were part white, it was natural enough to think they did not love their homeland as much as the pure Cherokee did. Also, the Treaty Party members tended to be richer than full bloods.

A peculiar quirk is that Major and John Ridge were full bloods, while Chief Ross was only one-eight Cherokee and spoke Cherokee so haltingly that when he addressed the council he needed help from an interpreter. He was completely Cherokee in feeling, though, and his full-blooded wife, Quatie, was much beloved among the people.

Brigadier General John E. Wool had been sent to keep the Cherokee under control, but he quickly saw that most of the trouble was caused by whites. When he tried to protect Alabama Cherokee, that state charged him with disturbing the peace. He was cleared of this accusation but asked to be relieved of his command on moral grounds. He wrote to the Secretary of War that the Cherokee were being terribly wronged and that "if I could . . . I would remove every Indian tomorrow beyond the reach of the white men, who, like vultures, are watching, ready to pounce upon their prey."

The election of Martin Van Buren as President was the finish to any chance that the Cherokee would be allowed to stay in Georgia. This little man, whom Davy Crockett is said to have described as being given to "strut and swagger like a crow in the gutter," announced, "No state can achieve proper culture, civilization, and progress in safety as long as Indians are permitted to remain."

When the May deadline came and the Cherokee went about their work as usual, General Winfield Scott was ordered to force them to leave. He had 4,000 regulars and 3,000 volunteers, but he wished to prevent bloodshed and suffering. He called the leaders together and told them their people must start west before another moon could wane.

Troops were all around and more were coming. "Will you then, by resistance, compel US to resort to arms? God forbid! Or will you, by flight, seek to hide yourselves in mountains and forests, and thus oblige us to hunt you down?" Scott pitied the Indians and ended his plea: "I am an old warrior and have been present at many a scene of slaughter; but spare me, I beseech you, the horror of witnessing the destruction of the Cherokees."

This appeal was printed on handbills and published in newspapers, as well as being handed out by soldiers throughout the Cherokee Nation.

Only a few families came in voluntarily. Many Cherokee wished to fight to the death for their homeland, but Chief John Ross urged against this.

On May 17 General Scott issued a general order to his troops, charging them to be "humane" in their collection of the Indians. No Indian should be fired upon unless he tried to fight. Horses were to carry the sick, old or disabled. No profane language was to be used, and the soldiers were ordered to be as kind as the necessities of a cruel task would allow.

Twenty-three stockaded detention camps had been set up throughout the Cherokee Nation. Every day troops would go out in squads to search the region and bring in all the Cherokee they could find. From these detention camps, the Cherokee would be sent to four main removal depots to start the journey west.

✳ On May 26 the soldiers began taking Indians wherever they found them. Since no preparations had been made, most of the Indians lost most of their household goods and belongings. John Ridge blamed John Ross for not warning the people to sell their livestock and furniture and get ready for the inevitable removal. As it was, the Cherokee were taken from their fields, or interrupted at meals or seized along the road. Women were ordered to leave their spinning, and children were gathered up in the middle of playing.

It was a cruel thing, even when done as mercifully as possible. Some soldiers and officers were rough and brutal, striking their prisoners or prodding them with bayonets. Sometimes children were separated from their families, and the Cherokee were often herded along like cattle with shouts and whoops.

Often the Indians had only the clothes they wore. Even before they were out of sight of their homes, white scavengers might break in to steal treasured family heirlooms, furniture, clothing, and drive off horses, cattle, hogs and sheep. They looted graves of jewelry and other valuables that the Cherokee buried with their dead, and sometimes fired houses and barns out of sheer vandalism.

About three hundred Cherokee hid out in the Smoky Mountains. One named Tsali killed a soldier. Scott was determined to prevent them from attacking his men and sent word that if Tsali would surrender himself for execution, the other hiding Cherokee would not be bothered. Tsali gave himself up and was publicly executed. The others of his group stayed hidden in North Carolina, where their descendants live to this day on the Qualla Reservation and put on a yearly pageant about the Trail of Tears and Cherokee history.

During June's hot, parching weather three detachments totalling more than 2,400 Cherokee were compelled to board boats that carried them up the Tennessee River to the Ohio, down the Mississippi, and to the Arkansas, which would take them to their future home.

By the middle of June the Tennessee River was

drying up till it was plain it could not carry boats and the next Cherokee would have to travel overland. This was going to be difficult, too, because a serious drought had dried up many wells, springs and creeks along the land route. Besides, the fever season had begun, and many people would get sick anyway without multiplying their problems by an arduous journey.

John Ross and other chiefs asked Scott to delay further emigration till cool weather. They promised to be gone before the end of October.

Scott was glad to agree. In July he met with Ross and the Cherokee Council and made an agreement. The government would let the Cherokee organize their own removal and provide $65 per person from which the tribe would pay for subsistence and transport. Thirteen thousand Cherokee had to move 800 miles overland. The region came alive with white contractors ready to profiteer off Cherokee misery.

Tons of food were needed, as well as 645 wagons and teams, drivers and interpreters. While these were assembled, the Cherokee lived in detention camps, crowded and in conditions that left them easy prey to sickness. That summer's drought brought hardship to everyone, but it was disaster for the Cherokee. They were wracked with epidemics. About five hundred died that summer in the camps.

Ross and the council had planned to move in thirteen detachments of a thousand each, beginning on the first of September, but the drought hung on till late in September, and it was impossible to start till the springs were replenished, which meant that winter travel could not be avoided.

One group of about seven hundred belonged to

the Treaty Party and would not move under Ross' control but set off by themselves in October, reaching Indian Territory in January, 1839.

Ross' supporters, the great majority of the nation, held a last council at Rattlesnake Springs, near what is now Charleston, Tennessee. Determined to preserve their tribal ways and pride as a people, they passed a resolution declaring that the Cherokee Nation's constitution, laws and customs would continue in full force. The Treaty of New Echota was again repudiated, and the law written down in 1828 confirming the old rule of death for any Cherokee who sold or exchanged tribal lands without power from the Council was solemnly reacknowledged. Of course none of Ridge's allies or any Western Cherokee was at this Council, but even if they had been, they would have been outnumbered.

The first detachment started out on the first of October. It was a bright beautiful day, but the people were full of grief as they set their faces to the west. The sick and old traveled in the rough wagons. Some rode horses and mules, and many had to travel on foot.

By early November twelve parties were on the road churned by hooves and wheels into a wretched quagmire now that heavy autumn rains had set in. Wagons sunk to the axles in mud, and exhausted, ailing Cherokee had to push and pull them free. River crossings were especially dangerous. In order to save money, the contractors usually overloaded ferries. One flimsy raft was sent across the Mississippi with double its safe load. It sank and almost a hundred people drowned.

Few of the Cherokee had been able to snatch up

any belongings that could increase their comfort. Most had only the single blanket provided by the contractors. Rain and snow stung them to the bone.

Besides the illnesses that struck them in the camps, new sicknesses daily killed the Indians. Pneumonia, tuberculosis, small pox and cholera ravaged the weakened travelers, so each stop was marked by graves. The physicians assigned to each group did their best, but malnutrition made the Cherokee easy victims.

Often they had only salt pork, corn, and coffee with molasses, for the contractors who had planned to buy most of the supplies along the way quickly learned that they were not the only ones eager to profit from the tragedy of the removal.

All along the way merchants and farmers charged outrageous prices for necessities. Contractors bought as little as possible in order to make money on their $65 per person. The contractors had planned to make the trip in eighty days, and as the time increased, their profits decreased. Their only comfort was that as the Cherokee died, there were fewer of them to feed.

The first detachment went northwest to Nashville, Tennessee, through western Kentucky, across the lower tip of Illinois, southeastern Missouri, and across Arkansas into Indian Territory. The other land detachments took about the same route but varied it to find game. Chief Ross with the thirteenth group traveled by water. His wife, Quatie, gave her blanket to a child and died of pneumonia.

In December, while the Cherokee died and suffered across 800 miles, President Van Buren told the Senate that they had migrated "without apparent reluctance" and with "happy effect." A Maine traveler who met several detachments of the Indians wrote in the New York *Observer* that he wished the President had been in the wet, freezing death-ridden camps of heartsick Cherokee to see with what "comfort and willingness" they were making the journey.

The dying and those too sick to travel even in the wagons had to be left along the road. Some were killed by ruffians and wild beasts, but most simply died of exposure.

Some white communities along the route gave the Cherokee what they could and treated them well, but more often tradesmen sold necessities at triple prices and others gathered to stare and mock at the weary Indians.

One Indian remembered how women, children, and even men wept when they left their homeland, bowed their heads, and started west. His father collapsed in the snow, rode in a wagon for one day, and then died and was buried near the trail. A week later the Indian's mother made one cry and fell dying. She was buried, and in the days that followed, all five of this man's brothers and sisters weakened and died. He thought probably all the Cherokee would die along the road. As he marched, he heard always the moaning and crying from wagons carrying small children, the sick and dying. Years later he said that he could still hear the constant weeping and cries of distress.

There was not a family which did not leave at least one dead loved person on the way. Four thousand people died out of the 13,000 making the journey, almost a fifth of the entire Cherokee Nation soon to be reunited in Indian Territory.

164

James Mooney, an early ethnologist who would years later study and describe the Ghost Dance, says that he was later told by one volunteer who had helped with the move, I fought through the Civil War and have seen men shot to pieces and slaughtered by the thousands, but the Cherokee Removal was the cruelest work I ever knew."

Still, the last group reached Indian Territory by March 25, 1839. They were kindly received and helped by the Western or Old Settler Cherokee, and those who had survived the Trail of Tears set about building new homes and beginning fresh.

But they had other affairs to settle. They had not forgotten or forgiven the Treaty of New Echota, and the horrors of the removal made them more set than ever on punishing the Ridges for what was seen as betrayal. Also, Ross' people felt that a united government should be set up over all the Cherokee, and since they far outnumbered Old Settlers and Treaty Party members, such a government would lead to Ross' dominance.

The Treaty Party had without question accepted the laws of the Old Settlers, who had no written constitution and only a few written laws. Twice a year they met in council to elect national officers, but it was a loose and fairly primitive system.

Since Ross' group had voted to bring its constitution and laws with them into the Territory, they were not happy to live under the Old Settlers' laws. Ross asked for a council to meet in June and unite formally the whole Nation.

About 6,000 Old Settlers and Late Immigrants, as Ross' group was called, met near what is now Tahlequah, Oklahoma, on June 3. Spokesmen on both sides said how good it was to be together again and how they hoped nothing would ever again divide them. John Brown, first chief of the Old Settlers, was about to declare the meeting over when John Ross asked him to state fully on what terms the Late Immigrants were being received and what privileges they had.

Brown willingly made another welcoming address to the newcomers. "We cordially receive you as brothers. We joyfully welcome you to our country." He went on to say that they could settle wherever they wished on land unclaimed by others, that they could vote and hold office, and that when the next elections for chiefs and judges, sheriffs and legislators were held, they could both vote and run for office. Of course this meant that the Late Immigrants would take over the government in time, but the Old Settlers did want their government to stay in power till the October Council.

Brown did agree that in order to handle claims and problems with the United States the Ross faction could retain its officials and call itself the Eastern Cherokee Nation. The attitude of the Old Settlers was generous and obliging, but it was known to the Late Immigrants that the Ridges and Boudinot were respected and liked by the Western Cherokee, gaining in influence, even though they had kept strictly out of politics. The Ridges and some of the Treaty Party had come to listen to the talks between the Old Settlers and Late Immigrants. But when this caused resentment among the newcomers who had so recently suffered and seen their loved ones die along the Trail of Tears, the Ridges had gone away.

The Late Immigrants hated the Ridges, believed them traitors, and wanted vengeance. No matter how reasonable and fair were the terms offered by the Western Cherokee through Chief Brown, Ross' group believed the Ridges were planning to work with the Western Cherokee to dominate the reunited Nation. Ross was determined to establish the constitution and laws of the Eastern Cherokee as those of the whole Nation, and he called on Brown to call a convention at once to draw up a constitution that would be voted on by all the people.

Brown again pointed out at the October council that the constitution and laws could be changed. When Ross would not wait till October, Brown adjourned the council and the Old Settlers went home.

Ross, however, kept the Eastern Cherokee in session to settle matters concerned with their removal. He was disappointed that a constitutional convention had not been called and that instead of being united, his people and the Western Cherokee were at odds. Still, when some of his faction angrily blamed the Ridges and predicted that they would continue to divide the Cherokee Nation, Ross warned his men against violence. He had always urged against revenge on the signers of the Treaty of New Echota, knowing that this would only lead to blood feuds that would waste Cherokee strength and leaders.

As the council was breaking up, some of the bitterest enemies of the Ridges held a secret meeting without the knowledge of Ross. The law was read—the one John Ridge had insisted be put in writing in 1829—which decreed death to unauthorized men who sold tribal lands. The principal signers of the

Treaty of New Echota were then judged, each by three members of his own clan. Major Ridge, who belonged to the Deer Clan, was condemned to death by three men of that clan. John Ridge, Stand Watie, Elias Boudinot, John Bell, James Starr and George Adair were all convicted in the same way.

Then numbers were placed in a hat, twelve of them marked with an *X*. Those who drew an *X* would be executioners. Allen Ross, Chief Ross' son, was not allowed to draw. His task was to stay near his father for the next night and day and try to keep him from finding out about the planned executions.

On the morning of June 22 John Ridge was stabbed to death in front of his wife and children; Elias Boudinot was tomahawked near Worcester's house; Major Ridge was shot from his horse; and Stand Watie escaped only because witnesses to Boudinot's murder sent him a warning.

Stand Watie swore vengeance and with a group of Ridge supporters prowled the region looking for assassins. Five hundred Eastern Cherokee gathered to protect Chief Ross, and the Cherokee Nation was in wild uproar.

In spite of this dangerous situation, Ross and his faction, known as the National Party, called a convention to meet near present-day Tahlequah on July 1. Ross felt that unless something was immediately done to unify the Nation, it would be torn apart by feuds and murders.

Two thousand Cherokee came to the convention, but only five of them were Old Settlers. One of these was Sequoyah, inventor of the syllabary, who served as vice-president of the convention.

This convention adopted an Act of Union, which joined the Eastern and Western Cherokee and provided for a national constitutional convention to be held in September. Amnesty was granted for all crimes committed since the coming of the Late Immigrants. This, of course, pardoned the killers of Boudinot and the Ridges. All signers of the Treaty of New Echota were declared outlaws unless they publicly confessed that they had been wrong.

Seven signers did this, but most insisted that making the treaty had been the only wise course and that Ross had caused most of the Cherokee suffering by encouraging them to stay in the East till they were forcibly expelled.

This split in the Cherokee Nation, caused by the U.S. government's insistence on removal, was perhaps as disastrous to the people as the Trail of Tears. For years to come, the Ridge and Ross factions would attack and avenge, each murder leading to another, till no one was safe.

After his convention, Ross sent a messenger with the Act of Union, the new constitution, and documents on amnesty and outlawry to a joint council of Old Settlers and treaty men. The messenger was refused, along with his papers. Though all Cherokee wanted peace, neither side wanted to place itself under the power of the other.

Treaty men appealed to the federal government to find and punish the killers of Boudinot and the Ridges and asked for protection from Ross.

General Matthew Arbuckle was instructed to find the murderers, but Ross claimed not to know whom they were; and though soldiers led by treaty men scoured the Cherokee Nation, they found none of the alleged executioners and the search was given up. Stand Watie would later kill a man who boasted of having shot Major Ridge, and many of the assassins died violently, but none was even tried for the killings.

Meanwhile, though almost no Old Settlers and none of the treaty men had approved the Act of Union, John Ross acted upon it and assumed power.

In June, 1840, a convention of Old Settlers accepted the Constitution, and in the same year two bands of Western Cherokee who had been living for years in Texas were driven out of that region and came to live in Indian Territory. Thus from 1840, except for a few hundred who remained hiding in the North Carolina mountains, all Cherokee lived together.

The Nation was still far from united. The feuds grew so bitter that President James Polk decided to separate the factions and give each its own land and individual government.

This prospect shook Ross, who above all wished to see his Nation unified and prospering. He worked for reconciliation with the Treaty Party, and in 1846, in Washington, leaders from the Treaty Party, Old Settlers and Ross' National Party all signed a new treaty. Even Watie and Ross shook hands and promised to forgive and forget their past conflict.

There was too much blood and hatred for old enemies to really trust each other, but both sides were exhausted and ready to settle at making new homes, farms, businesses and new lives. The underlying feuds would flare up again at the coming of the Civil War, but during the forties and fifties the Cherokee had a golden period of progress and became thoroughly at home in Indian Territory.

Their new constitution ruled that all executive, legislative and judicial officials must be blood Cherokees. Land was held in common. Individuals could build homes and use the earth for grazing and cultivation as long as they did not intrude on the rights of others.

A public school system was set up and supported by Cherokee educational funds provided for in treaties with the United States. There were eighteen public schools in 1843, and these steadily increased. Two seminaries for advanced study, one for young women and one for young men, were opened in 1851. Top scholars were sent to Princeton and other Eastern universities to complete their education. The Cherokee schools were far better than those for white children in the surrounding frontier.

Besides regular courts and peace officers, the Cherokee Nation had mounted rangers called Lighthorse Police who helped keep the Cherokee Nation free of much of the lawlessness common in the West.

The Lighthorse had been established by the Cherokee in their first written code in 1808. Lawbreakers had reason to fear them. The punishment for a first minor crime was a whipping of 25 to 30 strokes with green willow rods. A second offense brought 50 to 75 lashes, and the third meant an even 100. After the third crime, the court gave up trying to reform the accused and just had him shot.

The Lighthorse in Indian Territory had most of its trouble with intruding whites who bootlegged liquor to the Indians. Drinking was a heavy woe to the

Cherokee, and many Lighthorse died while trying to catch the men who made money from selling atrocious brews to the people.

Since U.S. citizens were foreigners in the Indian Nations and not subject to their laws, Lighthorse could not arrest white lawbreakers unless a U.S. Marshal was along. All Lighthorse police could do was escort white riffraff to the border and advise them to stay on the other side.

This impossible problem led the Cherokee to ask the Army to help control white thieves and bootleggers. Sometimes the soldiers caused more trouble than they prevented by their drinking and insulting or oppressive behavior to the Indians. In 1859 the Superintendent of Indian Affairs recommended that the whole Indian Territory be policed by a force of men from the Cherokee, Creek, Shawnee, Kickapoo, Delaware and other tribes living there.

This enlarged Lighthorse did a magnificent job till the outfit was done away with in 1902, when Indian Territory was submerged to become part of the United States.

Old-timers say that when an Indian was charged with a crime, he would voluntarily come into court and justice even if it meant his death. There were still hardened thieves and killers who fought it out with the Lighthorse in some of the bloodiest clashes of the frontier. When "Hanging Judge" Isaac Parker boasted that he was law west of Fort Smith (Arkansas), he was overlooking the potent law enforcement of the Lighthorse, who had infinitely more trouble with whites from his region than he ever did with Indians from theirs.

The Cherokee advanced in more peaceful ways,

too. Flatboats and steamers connected Cherokee towns with Fort Gibson, Fort Smith, and New Orleans. Roads were built and towns started while farms and ranches supplied an abundance of food, grain, horses and cattle. There were salt and lead mines. The Cherokee regained much of their former prosperity.

To their long list of firsts, the Cherokee added that of publishing the first newspaper in Oklahoma, the *Cherokee Advocate*. Most of its issues during the first two years carried reports of assassinations and murders arising from smoldering anger over the Treaty of New Echota and the Ridge murders.

The *Cherokee Messenger*, the first Oklahoma periodical, appeared in August, 1844. Also, Samuel Worcester had continued to print books, leaflets and the *Cherokee Almanac*, as well as the translation of the Old and New Testaments, which Boudinot had been helping with at the time of his ghastly death. Worcester had run to his dying friend and cried out, "They have cut off my right hand!" But still this brave and faithful friend of the Cherokee had continued his work. He had gone to jail in Georgia for aiding them, had followed them to Indian Territory, and even after some had killed his friend and helper, Worcester labored on.

As early as 1832 Jesse Chisholm, the famous Cherokee trailmaker, was trading with the Plains tribes in the western part of Indian Territory. The Cherokee were active in meeting with other tribes, including some of the Plains rovers, in efforts to have peace and friendship among all the Indians of the Territory.

173

Just as it seemed the Cherokee had won back their culture and prosperity, the Civil War exploded and blew apart the fragile Cherokee union. Located between Union Kansas and the Confederate South, the Cherokee Nation was squarely in the middle of the struggle.

Chief Ross tried with all his might to keep his Nation neutral. Black slavery was legal in the Cherokee Nation, though most full bloods opposed it and did not own slaves. Many mixed bloods did, however. These men, mostly wealthy and influential, had been Ridge supporters. They now favored the Southern cause, and Stand Watie organized a Cherokee regiment to fight for the South.

The Confederacy brought heavy pressures on Ross to join with it. At first he refused, but as Confederate victories made adjoining areas part of the South, neutrality became so difficult that late in 1861 Ross signed an alliance with the Confederacy.

The unhappy Cherokee Nation became a battlefield for Union and Confederate forces. In summer of 1862, overwhelming Union forces defeated Stand Watie and other Southern troops, captured the capital, and took Ross and other Cherokee officials prisoner. Ross was soon paroled and lived out his exile to the end of the war in Philadelphia and Washington. He encouraged the Cherokee to return to the Union. Many of his full-blooded followers joined the Union Army, and in 1863 Cherokee who favored the Union met on the Cowskin Prairie in the northern part of the Cherokee Nation. They repudiated the treaty with the confederacy, abolished slavery in the Cherokee Nation, returned the Nation to the Union, and elected a chief.

Since the Southern sympathizers had elected Stand Watie as their chief, there were now two Cherokee governments, each claiming to be the rightful one. Troops directed by these opposing powers fought each other through the rest of war in bitter fights across Arkansas and Indian Territory.

Their nation was occupied by Union forces, but this did nothing to check the most horrible kind of guerrilla warfare. People fled their homes to escape the ravaging troops and irregulars. Many did not come back till 1867. Then they found that whichever side they had favored, their houses and barns were burned, their livestock gone, and their fields and orchards destroyed.

Three Indian Home Guard regiments gave important help to the federal cause in the Indian Nations during the war. One regiment was mostly Cherokee and the Third Regiment was completely composed of "Pins," so called because of the crossed pins they wore on their coats. They served as federal scouts and were dreaded by Southern sympathizers. Members of Keetoowah, a secret society organized in 1859 to preserve Cherokee culture and independence, they had strongly been for abolition even before the war.

Stand Watie, the only Indian to become a brigadier general in the Confederate Army, continued to be highly effective with several hundred scouts and was the last Confederate general to surrender, June 23, 1865, in the Choctaw Nation.

The Cherokee Nation had lost about one-fifth of its total population during the Trail of Tears. The Civil War cost more. A census of 1867 showed that 7,000 Cherokee had died during the strife, one-third of the tribe! Saddest of all, many of these had died at the hands of other Cherokee.

It seemed that the white men not only had driven the Cherokee west, bitterly dividing their leadership, but had then forced them into the white man's Civil War. This had opened all the old rifts, deepened hatreds, started new ones, and beggared their nation.

That was not all. The United States dealt with the Cherokee as with a defeated foe, overlooking the fact that many Cherokee had fought for the Union and that their nation's alliance with the Confederacy had been almost forced. One price of being allowed to resume their own government was to permit the building of railroads across their land, a step that was bound to bring more whites to the region and lead to demands for Indian land to be opened to white settlement.

Northern and Southern Cherokee both sent delegations to Washington to negotiate the treaty with the United States, but the United States made its agreement with the Northern group led by Chief Ross. He died shortly after the signing in 1866.

His nephew, William Ross, a Princeton graduate and former editor of the *Cherokee Advocate*, served out the chief's unexpired term. The old feuds and divisions had grown deeper during the war, and the Cherokee split into the National Party, headed by Ross, composed mostly of mixed-bloods, while full bloods and former Southern sympathizers organized under Colonel Louis Downing in what became known as the Downing Party. Downing was elected principal chief in 1867 and managed to draw the factions together, uniting them to combat white invasion and regain their prewar prosperity.

By the eighties the Cherokee had rebuilt on the ruins. The Territory was full of good farms, ranches and stores. The railroads had brought new settlements and new markets for grain, foods, livestock, timber and stone. Tahlequah was known as a center of culture and education. Many Cherokee, better educated than most whites, went into law, medicine and education.

The rich grazing land in the Cherokee Outlet also brought both income and headaches to the Indians. Texas cattlemen let their herds pasture there on the way to market in Kansas. At first the Cherokee tried to collect grazing fees from each outfit, but this was so difficult that in 1883 they leased grazing privileges in the Outlet to the Cherokee Strip Live Stock Association for $100,000 yearly.

But the Cherokee Nation was not going to be allowed to keep these lands sworn to it so solemnly when the United States forced them to leave the East. Some of Oklahoma was opened for white settlement in 1889, and in that same year the United States began to press the Cherokee to give up the Cherokee Outlet.

Commissioners coaxed and argued till in 1893 the Cherokee Nation deeded 6,500,000 acres of the Outlet to the United States in return for $8,595,736.12. The vast area, best known as the Cherokee Strip, was opened to the greatest rush for claims in the history of Oklahoma in September, 1893. People who sneaked across the boundary ahead of time to stake the best claims were known as Sooners, which has become a nickname for people from Oklahoma.

The same Congressional act that ratified the Outlet sale set up the Dawes Commission, which

was to work at getting the Five Civilized Tribes—
Cherokee, Chickasaw, Creek, Choctaw and Seminole, all former dwellers in the East—to disband their
tribal governments, give up the holding of land in
common according to ancient tribal custom, and take
out individual land tracts. This would open the way
to turning Indian Territory, made up of the five
independent nations as well as several reservations,
into a federal state.

The Cherokee for several years would not even
talk with the Dawes Commission. The strong
Keetoowah were set against anything that would
weaken their tribal unity or give up more Cherokee
land. Two agreements between the commission and
Cherokee delegations failed, but in 1902 a third agreement was finally reluctantly approved.

Every man, woman and child of the Cherokee
selected 110 acres of average land from the tribal holdings. The Nation was merged with the state of Oklahoma in 1907, but its tribal government continued in
a limited way till 1914 in order to complete business
concerning tribal property.

Unwilling though they had been to see their
nation become part of a state, Cherokee were important in founding Oklahoma. Long experience in tribal
government had prepared them for responsibilities
and positive action. Several Cherokee were members
of the Constitutional Convention, and Robert
Latham Owen, a Cherokee attorney, was the first sen-
ator from Oklahoma, representing it in Washington
from 1907 to 1925. Other Cherokee served long terms
in the House of Representatives. A Cherokee was
elected justice of the Oklahoma Supreme Court in

1948. The great humorist Will Rogers was Cherokee. So was Rear Admiral Joseph Clark.

The Cherokee still have a principal chief. He is appointed by the President of the United States and gets no salary or expenses. It is an honor, but he has no power beyond personal influence. He does advise the tribe on suits before the Indian Claims Commission and works for their interests with the Bureau of Indian Affairs.

The Keetoowah Society has about seven thousand members, the majority being full bloods. Many of them live in rural communities and feel strong ties to old tribal ways and their relation with the earth and nature.

The society once included Christians and those who held to the old Cherokee faith, but when the Cherokee Nation was dissolved in 1907, differences grew deeper between the Christian and "Ancient" Keetoowah. The Ancient Keetoowah were so violently opposed to breaking tribal land into individual holdings that they withdrew from the main society once some members began dealing with the Dawes Commission.

These Ancient Keetoowah, dedicated to preserving tribal life and customs, became known as the Nighthawk Keetoowah because they met at night and were on guard against intruders. In 1932 about 120 families left the Nighthawks to form the Seven Clans Society. They favor common ownership and operation of the land, much in the old Cherokee tradition.

The Cherokee today live like other Oklahomans. They have tragic memories but great pride in their culture and heritage. Though many are successful in business, politics and the professions, thousands live in poverty on small farms in rocky, hilly country.

Development of weaving and basketry for sale has helped many of these poorer Cherokee, and improved soil conservation has enabled more of them to succeed with their crops. Their problems are the same as those of poor white families farming in the same region.

For over a century the Cherokee suffered from being more civilized than the whites around them. Now that they are full and active citizens of the United States, they can only benefit from their tribal identity and heritage.

FURTHER SUGGESTED READING

Debo, Angie, *And Still the Waters Run*. Norman, University of Oklahoma, 1984.

Foreman, Grant, *Indian Removal*, Norman, University of Oklahoma Press, 1976.

McLoughlin, William G., *Cherokee Renascence in the New Republic*, Princeton, Princeton University Press, 1986.

Report of the Select Committee on Affairs in the Indian Territory with Hearings (Volumes I and II). Washington, D.C., U.S. Government Printing Office, 1907.

Wilkins, Thurman, *Cherokee Tragedy*. New York, Macmillan, 1970.

Wright, Muriel, *A Guide to the Indian Tribes of Oklahoma*. Norman, University of Oklahoma Press, 1951.

INDEX

Trail of Tears, 147 ff., 175
Treaties, 15, 26, 38, 104, 116, 150,
 156, 162 ff.
Treaty Party, 157, 162, 165, 170
Tribollet, 90
Tucson, 79

Union States, 174-176
United States, 78, 103-104, 150,
 Army, 117 ff.
 Department of Interior 10,
 131-132, 141
 House of Representatives, 178
 Senate, 178
 Supreme Court, 154
 War Department, 83
Utah, 101, 118
Ute, 34, 111, 114-115, 118,
 123-124, 126-127

Van Buren, Martin, 158, 163

Wanderers, 16
War on Poverty, 145
Washington, D.C., 59, 71
Washington, George, 149

Washita River, 46
Wasps, 16, 17, 35
Watie, Stand, 155, 168, 170, 174,
 175
Webster, Noah, 154
Wessels, Henry, 65-66, 70
Western Apache, 76, 81-83, 84,
 89
Western Cherokee, 157, 162, 165,
 167, 169-170
White Mountains, 81
Wichita, 37
Woodenthigh, 54
Wool, John E., 158
Worcester, Samuel, 154, 157, 173
Wounded Knee, 37
Wovoka, 34-37

Yap-Eaters, 16
Yavapai, 76
Yellowstone River, 43
Yellow Swallow, 54
Yuma, 76

Zuñi, 76, 112

THE AUTHOR

JEANNE WILLIAMS was born on the Kansas-Oklahoma border in 1930. Her first book, *Tame The Wild Stallion*, which is still in print, won the 1957 Cokebury Award for Best Texas Juvenile. A member of the Texas Institute of Letters and a past-president of Western Writers of America, Jeanne has won four WWA Spur Awards for novels and the Levi Strauss Golden Saddleman which is given for a lifetime contribution to Western literature. Her books about the West have been translated into many languages. She lives in the Chiricahua Mountains of southeastern Arizona.